D1548355

# THE
# JESUS
# I KNEW

# THE JESUS I KNEW

## BY HUGH LYNN CAYCE

### Talks on Christ and the Edgar Cayce Readings

A.R.E. PRESS • VIRGINIA BEACH • VIRGINIA

## A Note to the Reader

The articles in *The Jesus I Knew* are edited lectures given by Hugh Lynn Cayce at A.R.E. conferences over the years. The editors have tried to retain the flavor of Hugh Lynn's lecture style as much as possible while making the talks more readable. Some of the Edgar Cayce readings may be slightly paraphrased or lack reading numbers since Hugh Lynn's lecture notes were not always available.

Copyright © 1984
by the
Edgar Cayce Foundation
All rights reserved

ISBN 87604-156-X

Printed in the U.S.A.

# Contents

# Foreword

Of the many sermons, lectures and books that I have read—except for the New Testament—nothing has stirred me more than Hugh Lynn Cayce's lecture on "Jesus Who Became the Christ." When Hugh Lynn spoke of Jesus there was a touch of reverence in his voice which was not apparent in other lectures. There was also an enthusiasm in the tone of his voice, as if he were not only convincing you, the listener, but himself as well of the astounding truths and activities of Jesus.

The Edgar Cayce readings declared that Hugh Lynn had been a follower of Jesus, knew Him personally, and then spent the major part of his life, after the Master's resurrection, spreading the teachings of Jesus.

For many years I had the privilege of traveling all over America and sharing the lecture platform with Hugh Lynn. No one who ever really knew Hugh Lynn would equate him with saintliness. But I have never met anyone in this life who made a greater effort in listening to and helping others, especially young people. Thousands of hours were spent listening!

If the patience he exhibited in counseling others is a key to heaven, then Hugh Lynn had the doors of heaven wide open! The readings state that patience is the cornerstone of all spiritual growth. And what takes more and greater patience than listening?

The Cayce readings also say that a sense of humor is a sense of balance. We recall from the readings that Jesus laughed even on the way to the cross. Perhaps the reader can find a parallel in the following story:

One evening Hugh Lynn and I were sharing a program in California. I was seated in the back of the audience and Hugh Lynn still further back. He got up to speak at the podium and, as he passed me, I noticed a rip in his trousers, glaringly spread open by his having his hands in his pants pockets. Quickly I took his arm and whispered, "Hugh Lynn, whatever you do, don't put your hands in your pants pockets because you have a rip in your trousers." He looked at me a moment, said nothing, but did remove his hands from his pockets. After the introduction by the master of ceremonies, Hugh Lynn walked to the podium, was silent for a long moment, then said, "Never in my life have I been better prepared to give a lecture." He then went on to relate very graphically the story of the discovery of the rip in his trousers. The audience was silent a moment and then exploded in a thunderous sound of laughter!

Just as Hugh Lynn had a truly wonderful sense of humor, so he also showed that he had a temper. On more than one occasion I was the recipient of his anger, but I must also quickly add that not once in the 40 years that I knew him did he fail to apologize. And again, from the readings: "He that never is angry is worth little, but he that is angry and controlleth it not is worthless." (1156-1) To me, his humility in apologizing every time he lost his temper was a saving grace.

Hugh Lynn's insight into the nature and life of the Master often awakened within the listener a sudden expansion of the meaning and teachings of Jesus. It was as if his understanding of the Master was transferred to the audience and a sudden greater understanding flooded the consciousness of the listener.

Again from the readings, we are given insight and understanding into the glories of awakening to the truth, for truth is "that which makes aware to the inmost self or the soul the Divine and its purpose with that soul." (262-81)

In all the years I knew Hugh Lynn, I often noted a remarkable sense of humility regarding his readings. Never did I hear him speak of any of his own exalted positions in his past lives that the readings revealed. Instead I heard him tell of his revelations regarding past lives in which he was a slave boy, arrogant and hard-headed! For the major portion of his life, when on the lecture platform, he referred to his father as "Edgar Cayce." Not until the latter part of his lecture career did he say, "My father, Edgar Cayce."

Hugh Lynn was, in my opinion, especially good at answering questions related to Christ or early Christianity. On one occasion, following a lecture and during the question period, a young lady stood up and said, "I am Jewish. I have also just joined an A.R.E. Study Group and I have a problem. I don't know what to do with Jesus!" An unusual silence fell upon the audience as all waited for the answer. Hugh Lynn said very slowly, quietly but firmly, "We the Gentiles accepted Him, a

Jew. So what is *your* problem?"

There is no doubt that Hugh Lynn loved life and that he was very human. He had his favorites as did Jesus, but unlike Jesus he did not always measure up. The thousands of hours that he spent counseling the young with whom he had a special rapport was a great plus in his life. (Remember Jesus and His love of children?)

Hugh Lynn's family, especially his wife Sally, was always most dear to him. One morning in 1981, Hugh Lynn stopped me as I was passing his office and related this dream to me. In the dream he was visited by the angel of death who told him that Sally, his wife, would be taken first. Hugh Lynn argued with the angel of death, begging him to take him first. The angel withdrew without comment.

As events in his life unfolded, it appears that Hugh Lynn convinced the angel, for he passed over on July 4, 1982. As much as Hugh Lynn loved life, he loved Sally even more, and she is still with us.

My husband Bill and I visited Hugh Lynn often while he was hospitalized and only once did he ever complain. As a nurse, I knew he must be suffering terribly and at times beyond description, but his endurance was even greater.

In conclusion, I will relate an experience at which I was present.

This occurred many years ago in the Dallas, Texas, home of Rudolph Johnson, who for many years was lawyer and counselor for the A.R.E.

Hugh Lynn had become ill. He was running a temperature of nearly 104°F. He seemed to be suffering from a deep-seated chest infection. It was the last evening of our meetings and lectures in Dallas and the entire Study Group had gathered at the Johnson home for a farewell "get together." Hugh Lynn had decided to join the Group for the meditation. After the meditation period, he arose from his chair and began packing and carrying boxes of books in preparation for our departure the next day. Knowing what his temperature had been just an hour earlier, I protested, telling him he should go back to bed and take care of himself as we faced a long trip the next day. He did not even look up but just kept right on packing. I walked away thinking to myself, *"men!"*

About a week later, Hugh Lynn said, "Elsie, I owe you an explanation." He then went on to say that during the meditation period in the Johnson home he had suddenly become aware of a most brilliant light, which apparently someone had just turned on. Opening his eyes to confirm his feeling, he was astounded to see Jesus standing in a blaze of glorious light! Jesus was looking directly at him and laughing at him! Telepathically Jesus said, "Why are you so surprised to see Me? You are always telling people that I will heal them and I'm here to heal you." And so he was healed.

Hugh Lynn Cayce, a follower of Jesus, was in my opinion an ardent worker in the vineyard of his Lord and his lectures brought to me a heightened understanding of the Master, as I trust they will do for all who read this book.

*Elsie Sechrist*

# Introduction

Twelve years ago, I walked into Hugh Lynn Cayce's office for one of our infrequent visits. I was on my way back to school in Texas after having attended the annual A.R.E. New Year's Conference. I had worried that I might miss the opportunity of seeing him, since he had seemed so busy.

But Hugh Lynn always seemed to be aware of the needs of the young people who came to A.R.E. and was known for being available to them despite his busy schedule. So when I went to make an appointment through his secretary Norrene, I was surprised to find that he once again had time to visit with me.

I remember how he looked as I walked in. He was sitting in front of his desk by the radiator, dictating letters for Norrene. The window was slightly open, even though it was nearly freezing outside. He liked the fresh air, he remarked. His executive's chair looked unused and rejected behind his desk. In fact, I thought to myself that I'd never seen him behind his desk, except when he had to take a telephone call.

He seemed especially jovial, even radiant, that day. Maybe he had sensed what I had on my mind. In the four years that I had known him, I had never just sat and talked to him about his relationship with Jesus. I wasn't about to wait any longer.

Maybe it sounds strange that I would want to talk with him about *his* relationship with Jesus. But I wasn't alone in thinking that Hugh Lynn *knew* something that he rarely divulged. He would hint at it and from time to time throw out an experience or comment which made everyone realize that, for him, Jesus was right here and right now. As we began to talk that day, I began to open up to him more than I had ever done before, telling him especially about the times I'd encountered Jesus in my dreams. In response, he began to share experiences with me, always prefacing the story with "I'm sure I've told you about this already." But he hadn't, and I urged him on. The hour flew. When I left his office, I found that for three days afterward I felt Jesus' presence so powerfully and tangibly that I regretted having to go to sleep at the end of the days. It was an undeniable Presence; and I haven't encountered it since.

I know several people who were fortunate enough to have a similar experience after spending time with Hugh Lynn. Was it some particular thing he said? I think not. I can remember few of the things he said to me that day. But I can remember his laughter, his radiance, and his love for Jesus. I have come to realize that Hugh Lynn's *mystical relationship* with Jesus was his most important teaching tool. Through it he was able to convey, on an emotional and intuitive level, what it was like to encounter and serve the Master directly.

From my experiences with Hugh Lynn, I have come to feel that in order to understand his approach to Jesus and His teachings, one need only analyze his mystical relationship with Jesus. On a rational level this relationship can be described as a set of simple but extremely bold propositions.

First of all, Hugh Lynn lived as though Jesus might appear any moment. To him, Jesus was an imminent Presence to those who served His purpose in the world. No matter what Hugh Lynn was doing—whether it was meditating or playing bridge—there was an air of joyful expectation that Jesus might at any moment walk into the room. This confidence was rewarded on many occasions, some of which he probably never shared with anyone. But his lectures are sprinkled with stories of such direct encounters.

Hugh Lynn believed that he was blessed with such encounters because he was simply trying to serve the Master's purpose in the world. In fact, his confidence in Jesus' accessibility seemed directly related to his confidence that he was doing God's work as best he could understand. However, the concept of his own perfection had no place in Hugh Lynn's mystical relationship with Jesus. He accepted that he was only expected to try his best, even if he fell flat on his face from time to time. He was the first to admit that his penchant for anger, for instance, often impeded his ability to serve; and he made a lifelong commitment to harness his fiery temper.

One cannot fully appreciate Hugh Lynn's mystical relationship with Jesus without also understanding the role of the "Light experience" in Hugh Lynn's life. From time to time, while he was in deep meditation and prayer, Hugh Lynn was infused with Light and incandescent love. Though he was cautious about mentioning such experiences, he occasionally spoke of this Light as something "one would crawl across the

United States" to experience again. He also said on several occasions that if one had to ask himself, "Did I experience the Light?" then the answer was "No." It was just that powerful to him.

How did Hugh Lynn's personal relationship with Jesus relate to his reverence for the Light experience? The two phenomena were inextricably related in Hugh Lynn's life; for they brought to him the same sense of renewal and faith. So it is not surprising that Hugh Lynn came to speak of Jesus' resurrected body as a body of Light and energy that was able to manifest itself anywhere in time, space and human experience. Later in his life, Hugh Lynn often spoke metaphorically about how he believed this "Body" was presently approaching the earth, as would a comet or a brilliant meteorite. In essence, Hugh Lynn agreed with the ancient Gnostic Christians, who believed that the resurrected body was an orb of white light.

Hugh Lynn never claimed that the Light was the sole province of Christianity. To the contrary, he felt it was the single unifying element in all of the world's religions. He concurred with the readings in regarding it as the Promise from which we had fallen and to which Jesus had been the first to return. In a deeply mystical sense, Jesus had become fused with the Light/Christ. Thus, for Hugh Lynn, the Light was also a Person.

In the final analysis, Hugh Lynn believed that these direct encounters with Jesus and the Light were available to anyone who gave himself to the task of serving others. It was just that simple. But it would be a mistake to assume that Hugh Lynn served others only in order to gain access to a particularly intense and satisfying inner experience. No, the mystical union and the commitment to others were inextricably bound together in Hugh Lynn's life. One fed the other, and neither assumed the greater importance. It was not surprising, therefore, that Hugh Lynn's spiritual life became more and more personalized as his commitment to others grew; and his service work became more and more powerfully transpersonal as his commitment to Jesus grew.

For me, nothing illustrates Hugh Lynn's fruition in his commitment more than when an A.R.E. staff member overheard him saying something to himself. Standing in the Headquarters lobby just two months before his death, he said with a sense of goodbye, "I love you all."

There have been many instances over the past few years when Hugh Lynn's approach to Jesus has had a clear impact on my life. For example, in one of my dreams, I found that I could fly. Delighted with my new-found freedom, I took off and flew around, only to fall eventually to the ground. As I picked myself up, Hugh Lynn walked up with a tolerant but sober expression. He said, "I'd hoped you would have gotten over your bent for these experiences by now. For *He* has been here twice already." I awakened with a start, realizing who "He" was.

For me and countless others, Hugh Lynn's approach to Jesus and His teachings imparted a very simple truth: He's right here and right now, if only you'll set yourself aside long enough for Him to get through to you.

I can't help but think that when Hugh Lynn crossed over to the other side and asked "How did I do?" he met Someone whose smile alone said what he already knew.

*G. Scott Sparrow*

# Faith and Miracles

I'd like to begin by quoting a definition of faith from Book I of *A Search for God.* This book was compiled from readings, given for the purpose, by Edgar Cayce and, as you may know, this two-volume series of spiritual concepts is now used by Study Groups all over the country. "Faith," this lesson begins, "is an attribute of the soul. It is the inner spiritual knowledge of the Creative Forces of the universe."[1] Then it goes on to examine the preparation necessary for the development of faith. This cannot be taught or forced, neither can true faith ever be destroyed. "Through the exercising of faith, we are able to give enlightenment to others. Let the mind be in us that was in Jesus the Christ; then there will come faith that is sufficient unto every need; even that faith which removes mountains, changes the destiny of nations, yea, and even brings worlds into existence."[2] Let the mind be in us that was in Jesus the Christ. The lesson concludes with a quotation from Hebrews, illustrations of faith from the Bible:

"And what shall I more say? For the time would fail me to tell of. . .the prophets; who through faith subdued kingdoms, wrought righteousness, obtained promises. . . And these all having obtained a good report through faith, received not the promise: God having provided some better thing for us, that they without us should not be made perfect; wherefore, seeing we also are compassed about with so great a cloud of witnesses, let us lay aside every weight, and the sin which doth so easily beset us, and let us run with patience the race that is set before us, looking unto Jesus, the author and finisher of our faith." (Hebrews 11:32-39, 40; 12:1, 2)

Here I should like to illustrate from the New Testament some further references to faith which help to define it. It is never enough to take the superficial meaning of a word for granted; words too often become mere labels. Here, in the word "faith," it is only after we have seen it in action and responded to its effect that it achieves its true purpose. In this light, let us consider

---

1. *A Search for God,* Book I, p. 47.
2. *Ibid.,* p. 49.

faith as it is used in the Gospel of St. Luke: "And the apostles said unto the Lord, Increase our faith." (Luke 17:5)

Where else will you find a more blunt, straightforward use of the word? Here it takes on a luster that is almost visible; there is wonder to it, a promise of limitless benediction. And though Jesus' reply may not be as familiar as His teachings on the Mount, it is touched with the miraculous: "If ye had faith as a grain of mustard seed, ye might say unto this sycamore tree, Be thou plucked up by the root, and be thou planted in the sea; and it should obey you." (Luke 17:6)

I don't know of any more vivid word-picture than the one this brings to mind—and at the same time so astringent. It revealed to the Apostles with startling simplicity that they had yet to put to full use the faith they already had, no matter how little it seemed to them; it gave them a yardstick by which to measure the intensity of faith, an intensity that makes possible the impossible.

Now we turn to the Gospel of St. Matthew, and here Jesus is speaking again: "Wherefore, if God so clothe the grass of the field, which today is, and tomorrow is cast into the oven, shall he not much more clothe you, O ye of little faith?" (Matthew 6:30)

Again in Matthew, let us weigh the words of a centurion, who understood authority in his own right as an official who both wielded it and answered to it. When told by Jesus that He would come to his house to heal his servant sick of the palsy, he replied: "Lord, I am not worthy that thou shouldest come under my roof: but speak the word only, and my servant shall be healed." (Matthew 8:8) Here is a blind acceptance of faith, a supreme and unshakable trust in it, asking no proofs. How did Jesus answer? His first words were to the multitude about Him. "Verily I say unto you, I have not found so great faith, no, not in Israel!" And then, to the centurion: "Go thy way; and as thou hast believed, so be it done unto thee. And his servant was healed in the selfsame hour." (Matthew 8:10, 13)

This is faith in its simple, unadorned, pure essence.

Call to your mind the luminous picture of Jesus as He comes down from the Mount of Transfiguration. He has been accompanied by a chosen few of His disciples, and on the Mount He had spoken with Moses and Elias. The disciples had seen the apparitions of these two great prophets conversing there with Jesus—the symbolic trinity that underlies all spiritual manifestation. And as these three were standing there together on the mountaintop, Jesus too had become transfigured, aglow with light; this radiance of the Spirit had poured from all three of them. In His mortal form Jesus now rejoined the rest of the disciples on the plain, where they had been working with a child who was possessed of a "devil." He was demented, and they had been trying, unsuccessfully, to heal him. Yet Jesus had taught them how to heal. He had taught them the power of faith. They were His chosen disciples; yet they had failed to heal this child. They asked Him why, and He answered very simply. But He also struck a chord that is common to us all: "Because of your unbelief. . ." (Matthew 17:20) And we shall find this again and again, when acts of faith have failed. It is your unbelief—the cause is your unbelief.

In this particular Gospel we are given another variation of the illustration of the sycamore tree: "If ye have faith as a grain of mustard seed, ye shall say unto this mountain, Remove hence to yonder place; and it shall remove; and nothing shall be impossible unto you." (Matthew 17:20)

Let us move ahead, until we come to the occasion when the Master returned to Nazareth, to His own community. We see Him enter the synagogue, and there He proceeds to read from the law and to preach to the congregation. In a few moments they are ready to throw Him off a cliff outside the city! Because of their unbelief He could awake no response in them. Faith would not operate, not even Jesus' faith, at this point.

You may say: "Well, it can only be that He withheld God's grace from them because of their arrogance. Perhaps it was a curse on Nazareth." No, it was not. The only thing Jesus ever "cursed" was a fig tree—if "curse" is the correct translation from the original Greek; I think it far more likely that the fruit of that fig tree was poisonous to ordinary men, carrying diphtheria perhaps, so He shriveled the tree in the same way that we would destroy contaminated food. No, Nazareth was not cursed. It paralyzed itself with its own unbelief.

Let us move on now to the question of healing.

Healing is a pure action of faith. All the miracles of healing arise out of faith alone: They are perfect examples of direct help from God, His direct answers to any prayer that has been given in absolute faith that it will be answered.

Most of us would be mightily pleased with ourselves if we could perform even the humblest of miracles. If we could pull off just a pint-sized miracle, we would feel that half the battle was over!

In the book of Genesis miracles used to come quite naturally to the patriarchs of that time: "So Abraham prayed unto God:

and God healed Abimelech and his wife, and his maidservants; and they bare children." (Genesis 20:17)

Suppose, for a moment, we come right up to the present day. Can we find signs of modern miracles here in our own midst? One's first reaction is to say: No, more's the pity. But let's take something as practical as artificial respiration. For years, tens of thousands of lifeguards on beaches and Boy Scouts pulling children out of ponds and ambulance attendants at the scenes of accidents were taught to restore respiration by kneeling on the subject's back and staving in his rib cage. If that failed—and it wasn't infallible!—they would use the poor fellow's arms as pump handles. Today every important first aid service in the country, including the Red Cross, has adopted the simple method of breathing into the lungs through the mouth. If the rescuer is carrying equipment, the process is made even more effective by a device which is placed through the mouth into the throat, obviating direct mouth contact. This method has saved lives time and again, lives that would have been lost by the old routine of "all hands to the pumps."

If this seems a rather ordinary, everyday kind of miracle, you have to remember that most of us possess a rather ordinary everyday faith. Our faith has to filter down to us, as it were, through our rather skeptical and very materialistic outlook on life.

If we had lived in the time of Jesus, the filtering system wouldn't have confined our vision. We would have seen miracles happen so often that we would have been in danger of taking them for granted.

"When he was come down from the mountain, great multitudes followed him. And, behold, there came a leper and worshipped him. . ." (Matthew 8:1-2) Imagine yourself in the midst of that multitude. Leprosy must have been an unattractive disease to push up against in a crowd. It is a literal wasting away of the body, a physical disintegration of the tissue. If it were suddenly healed, the results would certainly show. "And (the leper) worshipped him, saying, Lord, if thou wilt, thou canst make me clean." Listen to the utter belief in the leper's voice. He has the same inner understanding of faith as the centurion; he is convinced it is real. "And Jesus put forth his hand, and touched him, saying, I will; be thou clean. And immediately his leprosy was cleansed." (Matthew 8:2-3)

The belief came *before* the miracle, not after. Jesus was responding to faith here, faith as defined in *A Search for God*, an inner understanding of the law. The leper only makes the suggestion to Jesus; he doesn't make the flat request of the centurion, ". . .speak the word only, and my servant shall be healed." The centurion believed, but he still needed to be convinced that it could actually happen. The leper was already convinced *before* he spoke; his faith was whole and absolute.

Suppose you had been standing beside two blind men. "And when Jesus departed thence, two blind men followed him, crying, and saying, Thou son of David, have mercy on us. And when he was come into the house, the blind men came to him: and Jesus saith unto them, Believe ye that I am able to do this? They said unto him, Yea, Lord. Then touched he their eyes, saying, According to your faith be it unto you. And their eyes were opened; and Jesus straitly charged them, saying, See that no man know it. But they, when they were departed, spread abroad his fame in all that country." (Matthew 9:27-31)

Would you have wondered why Jesus told them to keep the miracle to themselves? He had made no secret of His healings. It was hardly likely to have been a psychological trick—if you tell somebody not to do something, he'll immediately go and do it; most of us have that little failing. But suppose the blind men had been sent by His enemies, in the hope that He would fail to heal them? His enemies needed all the proof they could get that He was a charlatan. Jesus, knowing this, still healed the two men because their faith justified it. But He did *not* heal them to make His enemies feel small. The least of His concerns was that His enemies be discomfited; so in effect He was saying, "Keep the healing to yourselves; don't use it as a challenge to My doubters."

While we are considering the miracles which have to do with tangible physical deformity, suppose we follow Him when "He entered again into the synagogue; and there was a man there which had a withered hand. And they watched him, whether he would heal him on the sabbath day; that they might accuse him. And he saith unto the man which had the withered hand, Stand forth. And he saith unto them, Is it lawful to do good on the sabbath days, or to do evil? to save life, or to kill? But they held their peace. And when he had looked round about on them with anger, being grieved for the hardness of their hearts, he saith unto the man, Stretch forth thine hand. And he stretched it out: and his hand was restored whole as the other." (Mark 3: 1-5)

Here you sense an almost negative use of His power. In the synagogue, on the Sabbath, He was watched by men who were anxious to see Him break the established law. In this case He *did* take their attitude as a challenge, because He was dealing with a moral issue. What more fitting place for God's will to be done than in the synagogue, *on* God's day? If His act had been "evil," against the law, surely God's hand would have prevented the miracle. But the miracle *had* happened, before their eyes. The energy that is used here, the defiance of false doctrine, is the dominating factor in this healing.

Which brings us to that very famous example: "And as he entered into a certain village, there met him ten men that were lepers, which stood afar off: and they lifted up their voices, and said, Jesus, Master, have mercy on us. And when he saw them, he said unto them, Go shew yourselves unto the priests. And it came to pass, that, as they went, they were cleansed. And one of them, when he saw that he was healed, turned back, and with a loud voice glorified God, and fell down on his face at his feet, giving him thanks: and he was a Samaritan." (A Samaritan was of low caste in Palestine; he came from mixed blood.) "And Jesus answering said, Were there not ten cleansed? but where are the nine? There are not found that returned to give glory to God, save this stranger. And he said unto him, Arise, go thy way: thy faith hath made thee whole." (Luke 17:12-19)

This is faith in terms of grace. The Samaritan's faith did not end with his request, nor in the healing; it was still manifesting itself in gratitude, in giving glory to God. Is this where so much faith fails? In the inability to give glory to God, the tendency to receive His gifts ungraciously, as no more than our due? Is this what happened to the disciples Jesus had taught to heal? Is this why many of them, many times, failed? Because they had taken the precious gift for granted?

Peter at the door of the temple, you remember, said "Silver and gold have I none; but such as I have give I thee: In the name of Jesus Christ of Nazareth rise up and walk." (Acts 3:6) And straightway, the man was healed.

So, not all His disciples failed Him. His teaching could even stretch out after His death and touch the unbeliever Saul on the road to Damascus. This Saul who became Paul was illuminated by a tremendous faith for a Christ whom he had never seen, for a Jesus he had mocked and persecuted. Yet the faith that was given him was mighty enough to establish the early church throughout Asia Minor. There is an old saying that no established member of a religion is ever so fanatic as a convert to it. Paul went at his task with a gusto he might not have had if he had been one of the original disciples. He seldom beat about the bush or slept on his decisions before he made them.

You may remember the incident when a magician performing before a crowd in the street objected to Paul's stealing his thunder with his preaching. The crowds had moved over to Paul and the wizard objected volubly. Paul's answer was brief and to the point. He said, "Shut up!" and it worked like a charm. Well, of course, it *was* a type of charm. The wizard was struck dumb. Maybe you could call it suggestion or hypnotism. Whatever it was, it packed a punch.

Even venomous snakes weren't immune to Paul's powers of suggestion. He was gathering sticks to build a fire when he was bitten by a lethal viper, and death was supposed to be in a matter of moments. If anyone died in this case, it was the viper. Paul shook it off and went on building the fire. All his concentration, you see, was on spiritual things; that is the point. He had just assured his flock that they were all going to be saved. And they *were* saved. The fire he was building, if you recall, was to warm the survivors of a shipwreck. That was symbolic in itself.

Paul could heal, he could do a remarkable number of things, because of the *intensity,* the *concentration* behind his faith. This is a man, not particularly young, who was beaten to a pulp in every city in Asia Minor, thrown out on the garbage dump and left for dead. What did he invariably do? He got up and walked away; and he *kept on* walking until all his churches were established and open for business. This bridge of faith which spanned the miracles of this man's life didn't begin with Jesus; it began before Him, and bridged His time, and it continues unbroken down through the ages until it becomes our concern, here and now.

One of A.R.E.'s books is entitled *That Ye May Heal.* It doesn't say that *Paul* may heal, but that *ye* may heal. It says that *you* can be the channel for the same spiritual power that Jesus used, that Abraham used, that Paul used, and that Peter used. It strikes at the heart of our present-day doubt about faith and miracles, and it offers many answers.

What does Edgar Cayce say about the miracle of healing through this faith, this exercising of an inner knowledge of spiritual law? Let me give you just three brief illustrations. The first had to do with the conditioning phrase, "according to thy faith."

"Please tell us," Edgar Cayce was asked, while he was in receptive sleep, "to what extent [543] has been benefited and just how we should continue treatments of this body."

This questioner belonged to a group which was studying

healing according to the principles set forth through Edgar Cayce. "Just how much has this body benefited, and how has he *been* benefited?"

"This has been aided," Edgar Cayce answered, "according to the faith as has been aroused in the body. . ." (281-5) Apparently, the healing in this instance is dependent upon the amount of faith, an inner understanding of the law, which can be aroused in this person.

He then informed them that if the group members employed concerted prayer and then the laying on of hands, they could bring about a complete cure for the person concerned.

In a similar vein, Edgar Cayce speaks of the structure of the body—in very inadequate language from a scientist's viewpoint, perhaps, but indicating scientific concepts which could give us some grasp of the necessary conditions under which a miracle might take place. Like many of our blessings, it could well be that miracles are all about us, if we had but eyes to see. We neither recognize nor understand them while they are happening right in front of our faces. Either we have lost faith, or we haven't enough of it—even as a grain of mustard seed.

Edgar Cayce says in another reading, ". . .let's analyze healing for the moment, to those that must consciously—as this body [the person who submitted the question]—must see and reason. . . Each atomic force of a physical body is made up of its units of positive and negative forces, that brings it into a *material* plane. These are of the ether, or atomic forces, being electrical in nature as they enter into a material basis, or become *matter* in its ability to take on or throw off." It is probably this ability to take on or throw off that is the secret of the healing process, as he indicates next: ". . .a group [of people working together] may raise the atomic vibrations that make for those positive forces as bring divine forces in action into a material plane, those that are destructive are broken down by the raising of that vibration! That's *material,* see? This is *done* through *Creative* Forces, which are God in manifestation!" (281-3) A group may thus raise those atomic vibrations which make for positive forces.

"Hence, as self brings those *little* things necessary. . .for position, posture, time, period, place, name, understanding, *study* each, and assist each in [his] respective sphere. So does the *entity become* the healer." (262-3)

Another request made was: "Please clarify our minds as to the method and way for us to proceed in seeking to help others." These were people, fumbling like you and me in their efforts to understand the law, to try and increase their faith and to bring this in some small way to the aid of others.

"Grace, mercy and peace, is given to those thou asketh for in the proportion as thy trust, thy faith, is *in* Me." (281-2) He is saying this as he would paraphrase it from one of the statements of Jesus to His disciples.

"Is there not some way of knowing," another questioner proceeds, "that results have been accomplished while treating a patient?"

"By their fruits ye shall know them. As there is seen the actual physical results in the lives that are aided in their consciousness, then these bring the actual physical results as viewed from a material mind. As has been given, by prayer, meditation, many a load has been lifted for a brother and friend." (281-6)

By continuing to concentrate upon what you, in your own experiences, have found to be blessings, from keeping His laws and His will and leaving the results with Him, or by faith in the power entrusted by the *activity* of that thought, you may see results.

When you pray, when you give a word of encouragement, when you speed a silent prayer for a child or a husband, a friend, mother or sister, or someone close to you, do you *expect* it to work, or are you mumbling in the dark? Do you actually believe that miracles *can* happen in our time, in our day, that you can be in some small manner a channel through which God can operate in the earth?

I think that we must learn *how* to be channels for this spiritual force. This is God's way, this is God in action, God's way for the universe.

It is easy to look around, to read the right books, to talk about wonders that happen to other people—but what about the little miracles that are part of your own life? I think even the wisest of us underestimate ourselves badly—we downgrade even the simplest things we do, a touch of a hand, a word of encouragement, a prayer for someone in trouble. "Oh, anyone would have done the same!" you say. I wonder!

It seems to me that the Edgar Cayce readings, indeed the whole purpose of our Association's concern with the tremendous mass of data at its disposal, centers in this area of challenge. We are being challenged to accept the possibility of miracles, which means we are being challenged to develop an inner understanding of spiritual law that will permit us to operate it. This Association for Research and Enlightenment has a very real reason for existence if it enables us to learn how to span the bridge between us and the strange outposts of psychic phenomena, parapsychology, all the unseen energies that affect us. Edgar Cayce left behind him a mass of data that covers an amazing range. It can teach us to harness forces which, when properly employed, will enable man to become a channel through which his less fortunate brothers can be helped.

The word *psychic,* as Edgar Cayce defined it, is not some outlandish jiggery-pokery with ouija boards, but the simple business of the soul in action, of spiritual law understood and applied to our way of life, to our actions, to our words and thoughts. Spiritual law *works*—and we can *see* it working!—within ourselves and within others who explore these areas. What is our prime, our foremost, concern here on earth? Isn't it the soul? Isn't it the need to understand the laws to which the soul responds, here, in its earthly embodiment?

This Association devotes itself to the study of these laws, the means whereby faith can be made manifest. Somewhere at the very end we reach the transformation, I think, of faith into the miracle.

I dearly wish that you and I could come to grips with this more intimately, in a hand-to-hand encounter as it were. Perhaps we are too content to dabble around the edges. Perhaps we are devoting too much time and energy to sticking pins into little wax images of one another. This can add up to a busy day. We can exhaust ourselves in trying to win, or lose, inconsequential arguments. This is why miracles come in small sizes today. Jesus has placed no more limitations on you and me than He placed on Paul. But Paul's miracles were vast enough to shake the earth.

Now all of us are gifted in different ways. If we do fling ourselves wholeheartedly into this acceptance of faith made manifest, we can't *all* become healers or ministers, teachers or seers. The response will be different in each person, some brought about through a word of counsel, some through a touch of the hand, some through the simplest of deeds of common kindness to the right recipient, at the right moment, and from the right motive. There are many footpaths to heaven; and I do not run the map concession. I'd be a fool to demand of you some particular talent that you don't happen to possess. But I *do* suggest that there is a force readily available which can transform *any* talent into a way of faith.

Jesus' earthly life ended with what must surely stand as the greatest miracle since the creation: His resurrection.

When, that morning in the garden, He warned others not to touch Him, He was saying in effect: "The substance of this new body of Mine is vibrating on a higher plane of energy than yours. So don't touch Me, I haven't yet polarized it; it would be safer for you to try and seize hold of a thunderbolt or a flash of lightning."

He appeared in this form again and again, all over Palestine, to prove to His disciples and pupils that the realm of spiritual law in which He now moved was the Reality, and *their* world of slower vibration was the Illusion, a brief, passing phase. In short, if you like to think of your life before you were born as the caterpillar stage, and the life you will inherit after death as the butterfly stage, then the shape you are in right now is the cocoon! Faith *is* matter, you see, matter manifesting at a higher rate of vibration than a pork chop or the end of your nose, but matter nonetheless, conforming to and governed by the same laws that govern your nose and the pork chop.

I'm sure you've seen someone try to walk through one of those sliding glass doors, thinking it was open when it was shut, and very nearly stunning himself in the process. The glass of that door is no less solid than the spiritual laws which govern faith. You may not be able to see them with the naked eye—but think twice before you try to barge your way through them!

Now do you feel you might be able to allow for the possibility of a world beyond this one; and that *this* one is only a faint shadow of the real one beyond? Or does it still make you feel a fool? A fool is quite the easiest thing to feel; anyone can do it! Some of us can do it without even trying! But if you *do* accept the existence of that other world, then you have accepted the existence of the resurrected body of Jesus: and that living, resurrected body radiates the energy of a tremendous power plant. If the *Nautilus* can operate for a generation on as much atomic energy as would fill a walnut shell, will you tell me what limits there are to the power radiating from the body of Jesus? As much as would cover the head of a pin would transform every hut and hovel and house on this globe into the bastions of Paradise, burning away the crust of unbelief under which we suffocate. *Nothing separates us from the radiance of that body, but ourselves, our unbelief. That's all!* That is why the aim, the purpose and the goal of this Association is to understand and then apply the spiritual laws that constitute a faith in Christ, a power that can and does and will illuminate our lives until, by their brightness, we see His miracles come to pass again.

What greater manifestations could there be in the inner soul of anyone in a material plane than bespeak those things of the Son of the Father in such a way and manner that those that hear may know that thou hast indwelling in thine inmost soul the knowledge of the Father, in the Son, and the *love* of the Father to the sons of men!                    262-58

# A New Commandment

"A new commandment I give unto you, That ye love one another. . ." (John 13:34) We forget so easily Jesus' admonition to love one another. Let's examine for a few minutes our concept of love, and how we need to work with it and deal with it in a much broader fashion.

"God is love." We hear the phrase so often that we lose the meaning. God is love. The law of love. There are many spiritual laws, but this one is perhaps the most important. Part of our problem in understanding and applying the law of love is tied up in our concept of God. You and I have a tendency to create God in our image. God made us in His image, and it has been said that we have been returning the compliment ever since. We've been making God in our image and giving Him our characteristics. So, if we think of God as love, then God's love becomes the way we love, and that understanding is fairly inaccurate as well as limited—and we know it. We cut Him down to size. Thus He has become for humanity at various times in history a god of wrath and destruction, a god who was greedy and demanding, a god in contest with other gods of the universe and who was overthrown, a god full of wrath and punishment. Mankind's idea of God was this kind of God.

With Jesus we come to a completely different picture of God, of God as the Father. He puts it very bluntly for us: "Which one of you who has a child who if the child were hungry and asked you for bread would give him a stone? Do you think your God is any less merciful?" (See Matthew 7:9.)

Yet we blame so much on God. I heard someone the other day talking about a whole pattern of suffering and failure, saying that it was God's will. This, to me, is an inability to see the goodness of God, the love of God. We attribute to God the same kind of attitudes that we hold onto.

In the Edgar Cayce readings we come face to face with a strange statement that will explain so much, if we will come to grips with it and admit that this is the condition: Mankind has chosen physical consciousness "as a diversion" from the real life—a spiritual state of awareness, a garden of Eden, if you will. A choice was made to move out of this state and to create a world of our own; thus, we had cut ourselves off.

Let's not lose sight of this point: that the soul has simply reached out into matter. We haven't, however, moved over *totally*. For a long time now people have been correct in saying that we are not all here! In this sense, there is only part of the soul in us. It's part of a reach, of a whole, but the consciousness has moved to the level of this three-dimensional plane. So, in this plane, we have shut ourselves off. We must move in consciousness back to where we can perceive the oneness of all force. Then, we can begin to relate to God as He really is and not as we perceive Him from a slowed-down, lower level of consciousness where we get things mixed up. When we get confused, we begin to maul and hurt each other because we are frightened. We're afraid we are going to lose something. We are so possessive. But you can't lose God; He has no intention of losing us! We only lose consciousness of Him.

So this concept of love is partly our way of looking at how we perceive God. We create God and perceive that He acts as we would if we were God. That is a very limited concept. As we move and expand our own consciousness, we come closer to God awareness.

Think about how we look at a human being. We look at the body and say, we are this. Now we know that this is not entirely true, but we act as if this body is all of us. We can't wait to get to the table; we think we're going to starve to death otherwise. We reach out to satisfy everything in the flesh, at the physical level, as if it were not inexhaustible. There isn't any lack—only our picture of it, our attitude about it.

We get caught up in the emotional life of anger, hate, fear, and lust and get confused by these emotions that are of a three-dimensional world. They are not wrong in themselves, but they just don't belong to us. We act as if we are going down to that level of consciousness rather than moving up to the level of God consciousness. We try to train our children not to fight, but look at the example we give them—we do a lot of fighting ourselves. We are caught up in our possessions and in our conflicts over those possessions.

Now when we think of the mind and its confusions, we can see how it would keep us from loving because it creates all kinds of strange patterns and desires. Frequently it is in conflict with our will. The will of the soul is to return to God consciousness, but the patterns that we create in the mind cut us off from our ability to love. That is *all* that cuts us off. Though we are created in the image of God, it is hard for us to see this because of the patterns we've built, the negative thoughts we hold about each other rather than seeing the God in others.

When we finally begin to deal with our exact concepts of love in the earth, we quickly realize just how silly we are. We get involved in physical love, which is a beautiful thing. "...all love is lawful, of every nature, not *all* is *expedient* unto good works." (1632-3) All love is beautiful, the readings say, but some of it is not expedient at a given time and place. You and I become confused and very selfish and egotistical when we get involved and caught up in physical love. When we add the mental and emotional patterns of our lives, then we *really* get involved, emotional, and possessive. Even with our children we beget possessive love that smothers, destroys and kills this love.

But when we begin to move toward a more universal concept of love such as Jesus manifested, we start to relate to God in a more real sense. There are several ways in which we can measure love.

First, how close does God walk with us in our daily lives? How personal is He to us? How close are we to Him? How often do we praise God, thank God, relate to God? Our efforts in prayer may bring this about. Through prayers of thanksgiving, praise and admiration, we can build a very personal experience with God.

Second, how do we, you and I, consciously try to make our will one with God's? Do we affirm this and open ourselves to His will, or do we say as St. Augustine, "Lord, make me pure—but not now." Are we asking to know God's will or are we trying to relate to it in opening ourselves, but not now—"Not Thy will in this situation." Are we saying, "Now, I'm willing in this way but not in this other way. Don't bother me over here. I want my will over here, but I want *Your* will about this over there." You see, we begin to measure it. What's God will? Do we stop to find out? How do we discover God's will? We've got to relate ourselves to it, to open ourselves to try to know what God's will is for us.

Now, the third way we can relate to God and God's love may sound rather Sunday-schoolish to you. It's in the words of Jesus, "If ye love me, keep my commandments." (John 14:15) It's that simple. Love is related to obeying the spiritual laws that we know. Now you don't have to obey what Susie knows. Susie may be way up on cloud nine and know a lot of spiritual laws. Let's say, for the sake of argument, that you and I don't know the laws Susie knows, so we can't follow those. But we have to follow the ones we *do* know. We have to obey them. We can't just know about them; we have to live them and put them into action. "If ye love me, keep my commandments." (John 14:15)

Fourth, we can understand love if we give. Now this hurts. Love is giving. We can give money sometimes, but we often can't take the time to give ourselves. We can't even take the time to listen to someone. You can give a child a TV set, but you can't have a conversation with him—you haven't got time. You can lend a friend a book, but you can't take the time to listen and encourage and care, to reach out and touch. Love is giving. What do we give? What do we have to give? Prayer, love itself, constructive thought, encouragement, the touch of a hand, a smile—these are the simple things of which we have so much. We can give them away, over and over, and never miss a one. You never miss a smile, a prayer, a kind word or a word of encouragement. This is love.

We also don't understand the law of giving money. It's partly our problem of rationalizing and, in a sense, of fearing a lack. I used to be so confused about this. It simply amazed me that when you give money away, you get it back. That's absolutely fantastic! It's the craziest thing! But, you know, it's the vacuum idea: The more you give away, the more you get. Give yourself and use all the opportunities you have to serve. These are all expressions of loving.

Now, the fifth concept: Love will know its own. Love in its expression brings about the movement toward God consciousness like nothing else does in our lives. The more we love, the more true is this. Even at the physical level, we've come to understand a shadow of this. The greatest physical ecstasy that we know is in the act of love, yet this ecstasy is pale in the light of the mystical experience for the body, the mind and the soul. Jesus spoke about this marriage, this union with God, which comes through loving. The ecstasy of this mystical experience also comes about through loving.

The last concept: the expectancy of His coming. I don't know how you feel about seeing or talking to Jesus. A relationship is love. When you talk to a friend, you meet a friend, you embrace, you care, you express. So you say, "Well, if Jesus is around anywhere, I haven't seen Him." Have you expected to see Him? "Oh," you say, "even if I saw Him, it would only be my imagination." How do you know? Would it really convince you if you saw Him suddenly? Expectancy is necessary for this experience.

Several years ago I suddenly knew that I had to go to a certain place. I knew He was there and that I could meet Him if I went. So, I took an A.R.E. tour to the Holy Land. One day as I stood on the north coast of the Sea of Galilee, still with this expectancy of seeing Him, I knew He was there. Now I *expected* Him and so, as the tourists were walking around with the guide, I walked away from them down to the shore. There was a light there. I walked into that light, and I was home. It was one of the most glorious experiences in my life. I went away from the light, got my wife Sally, and walked again into that light with her. We both knew we were in the presence of God.

This is as close as you can get to your expectancy, your willingness to love and give of yourself to His work in the earth. We have absolutely no excuse for existence in this earth except to love God and serve our fellow man. It's that simple. ". . .love one another." (John 13:34)

Don't underrate yourself. God looks on the inside, not on the outside. He deals directly with each and every one of us personally and individually. This is love, and this is grace.

By living under the law of grace, we begin to accept God's love and God's forgiveness. Everything is speeded up for us. The Edgar Cayce readings, as well as some of the great Hindu philosophies, say that you and I in essence have never left the throne of God except by projection, by movement in consciousness, by creating and moving into this plane and that the real part of us is still in the presence of God. That part has never left Him, yet you and I don't know it. Indeed this is maya, an illusion; it is not true.

God has already forgiven man, and everything that Jesus says points to that. But you and I have to recognize and accept that fact. Meditation makes it possible for us to begin to accept God's love, and, as we begin to accept God's love, we can begin to love ourselves and then others. There are several steps to do this.

1) "Be ye unhurt by hard words." This step is a tough one. The key is that you and I have got to try to learn how not to be hurt by hard words. You see, we resent this, because it is an attack on self. This is one step, and it ends with how to get to the throne of grace.

2) "Cry not peace when thou, thyself, hast not shown peace to thy brother." Show peace, bring peace—into a conversation, into a room, into relationships with people. How much time we spend contending, spreading contention and building contention! We wonder, then, why the world is full of it, when we build it in our own lives, we talk about it and share it with others. We stir up stories of contention; however, we can't find

and accept God's love in that state of mind or emotion. So show peace, bring peace.

3) This next step involves a breakdown on the word *righteousness*. "Thus find it in self. Know that so long as you feel there is karma it is cause and effect but in righteousness ye may be justified before the throne. Thus ye may pass from cause and effect or karma to that of grace." You and I have got to begin to perform right acts; this is righteousness.

4) "Creative acts." Some of you, who are expressive and creative in writing or in working with art forms of various kinds, find that you—without even knowing why—get so much release, so much healing of the self and of relationships, in doing that which is creative. Somehow it gives you such an opportunity to be free, to get rid of tensions, pressures, petty anxieties, fears, and hates. Creative acts, then, bring us under the law of grace. "No longer is the entity then under the law of cause and effect. . .but rather in grace." (2800-2) Our creative activity brings us into alignment with God's love.

5) "Choose according to ideals." If you want to be able to accept God's love, God's forgiveness, then begin to choose according to your ideals. Now, if you break this concept down and think about it a while, you'll understand why this is so. You cannot sell yourself short. This is the reason, I believe, that affirmations are such a challenge: They are statements of ideals and purposes which you constantly focus on and bring before yourselves. Some of you may fret about them and try to avoid them. But when you meditate, these affirmations—statements of your ideals and purposes—will demand a great deal of you. They will bring you constantly face to face with the necessity of choosing when to act, to choose according to the ideals that you hold. They will begin to straighten out many of the ways in which you may wiggle around the laws and get yourselves constantly tied up in knots.

6) "Forgiveness." If we are to accept God's love and forgiveness, you and I must learn how to extend these actions—and not just to others. Yes, it is very important that we love and forgive others, but you know that where we must begin is with ourselves. We must forgive the self; it's part of God, too. It's a soul, a being, a child of God, a creation. So many of us have more difficulty forgiving ourselves, and we're not even aware of it. What are its signs? They come under several guises: guilt, self-condemnation, and self-pity. When we begin to turn loose and forgive self, then we can forgive others and can align ourselves with God's forgiveness.

Meditation makes possible this kind of attunement; it helps us to bring ourselves into alignment. So, as we begin to discover ourselves to be indeed spiritual beings, then you and I must begin to act like spiritual beings and be able to forgive ourselves and others. For if we are gods in the making, we had best begin to act like it. This is one of the first, essential and necessary steps. I don't believe there is anything in all of the Edgar Cayce readings that makes this so possible as meditation.

# Jesus' Concept
# of His Fellow Man

And thou art thy brother's keeper. Not that ye should impose or impel another entity by thine own ideas, any more than God impels thee. For, He hath given thee the free will, the birthright, which is as the mind, that makes for the alterations. Hence ye may give expression even as He did, who came into the earth that we through Him might have eternal life.                                                        1747-5

Now there are several implications in this statement: First, we are our brother's keeper. The question is, "Who is our brother?" Jesus spells that out neatly in several places in the New Testament. The following reading outlines it pretty well, too:

Whoever, wherever he is, that bears the imprint of the Maker in the earth, be he black, white, gray or grizzled, be he young, be he Hottentot, or on the throne or in the president's chair. All that are in the earth today are thy brothers.                     2780-3

Then, we have another idea—not to impel or impose our ideas "any more than God impels thee." (1747-5) There is not a person who hasn't, at one time or another, grasped and held the idea that God is making us do something, is imposing something on us. When we run out of everybody else to blame for situations, we blame God. For me, the readings are explicit in this area: God does not punish; God does not impel or push man. He merely confronts man with choices. Sometimes these choices are as revolutionary and as "mind-boggling" as the one that came to Saul on the road to Damascus.

You and I are confronted with a challenge—to try to live up to a pattern and a standard that we see. And we likely say, "I can't accomplish that." Without His help it *is* difficult—and yet *with* His help He says, again and again, that we *can*, it *is* possible for the God in us to be awakened and to respond to the God in our fellow man. Unless we want a complete pattern of cause and effect to build up and overwhelm us, we had best back up and look at our responsibility in detail. God does not punish, and so, as the readings suggest, neither should we impel or push.

Jesus goes a lot further. He says, ". . .resist not. . ." (Matthew 5:39) *Resist not.* He doesn't say there isn't evil. He just says that the way to deal with it is not to resist it, not to fight back, not to get angry, not to be afraid. We must begin instead to shape and mold and work with our lives until we can apply the spiritual laws that we know, at an everyday level of thought and word and action.

The readings go on: ". . .accepting, believing, knowing then thy relationship to that Creative Force." (3508-1) You see, until we can begin to believe that God is a part of us, that we are a part of God, that we are part of a plan, the whole business of living is a very difficult trip. "For He hath called thee friend; not servant, but a friend, a brother, a sister. For 'Who is my mother, my brother, my sister? They that do the will of the Father in heaven, the same is my mother, my brother, my sister.'" (3508-1)

And then comes a sharp focus: "For he that loveth his brother, his neighbor, yea his enemy, is a brother to the Lord—the Lord who is the Son, who is the Savior, who is the spirit of truth and purpose." (3508-1) "A brother to the Lord" is a nice phrase. We can enjoy that kind of relationship. And we can have it.

"As these are applied in relationships to others we come to those questions that have been indicated; when ye shall stand before the throne of mercy, the throne of grace. 'Inasmuch as ye have done unto one of these, even my little ones, ye have done unto me.'" (3508-1) The *least* of these, my little ones. These little ones are multitudinous in the earth. Some of these little ones are tremendous and driving and forceful. Some of these little ones are all sorts of gods and have all sorts of faces and all sorts of religions and all sorts of racial backgrounds and characteristics. And some of these little ones have come out of a past where man has done much to man in the history of this world.

If, indeed, this concept of karmic patterns and memory is possible, how much healing, then, must go on, *must* go on now, if man is to survive. A pattern of peace in the earth is necessary. Forgiveness is the key—not only our forgiving, but accepting being forgiven.

It's hard for most of us to ask forgiveness of another, to say—even in our heads, much less in the midst of a confrontation—

"Forgive me." I did it the other day. I had been thinking some very nasty, aggravated thoughts about one of our staff members who had been doing things that I didn't think were appropriate and had been doing them very badly. I had spoken, I had remonstrated, I had suggested—and nothing was happening. It dawned on me that I had better back up and start over, because the situation was getting worse, not better. So I publicly apologized (not that I necessarily wanted to do it publicly but the opportunity to do so arose).

You and I have to reach a point where we can deal with our patterns and memories before they mount and build. We've got to be sensitive to all those things we've done that people remember. We need to be willing to be responsible for them, because there is not a lot of time. We have to re-establish our relationships, but we can't go back over each point bit by bit and dig it out and say, "Well, I did this and you did that." It isn't something between two people; it's something in the memory that's total.

We have to change ourselves. We have to love and express that. We have to be concerned and care, be patient and kind and thoughtful to re-establish, reaffirm the Divinity within us that relates to this other person. We call this dealing with the karmic memories in us and in others. We are our brother's keeper, and we cannot just say, "Well, I've done this and I've done this other since then. I'm not responsible for what I did then, I've changed." That "changed" business has got to be put into action. You can't just put on another suit of clothes—another binding for the book, as Benjamin Franklin put it—because the *you* is still the same. When people begin to react negatively, you say, "I'm not doing anything. Why are they treating me this way?" Yet you've already done it and it is in their memory. *You have to change so that they can begin to see that change is taking place.* It is not just up to them to change their negative emotion about you. You need to admit that you'd been acting the wrong way. They may be wrong in their concept of you now, but, if you are to be your brother's keeper, you've got to change their memory by replacing that negative in their minds.

Most of us are living with dozens of these situations in our homes and in our families and everywhere else. Memories of what we did when and where. There is an interesting case of a boy who had in a previous life been the father of his father now, and he'd beaten the daylights out of that one who is his father now. By the time he got here this time, his father had the belt ready. He remembered him, and they had one awful time. The individual responsibility is not in fighting back, but in the changing of the individual. In other words, the boy had to change his image by changing *himself* and expressing love and kindness and patience to his father; as well was it the responsibility of the father who remembers wrongly and who took advantage, for a time, of this small body to do the same.

Being our brother's keeper requires us to make changes in ourselves so that we can erase the negative thought patterns that exist in other people's minds. We change by being different: by forgiveness, by love, by patience, by kindness, by long-suffering. (Sometimes it *is* long-suffering in these relationships!) And this, again, is not karma *between* two individuals. Rather it is memory in an individual that you help them plant by being different, by showing them a soul that is awakened and following spiritual law, that is following the pattern of Christ's laws of love for others. It heals them and helps them to awaken also.

This, for me, is what Jesus was talking about when He said, ". . .resist not. . ." Don't fight, don't be angry, don't feel full of self-pity because this is imposed on you from the memories of people you knew when you did sin. ". . .go, and sin no more." (John 8:11)

We are working with the continuity of experience in life. As we gradually, a little here, a little there, line upon line, precept upon precept, begin to bring ourselves into alignment, this spiritual being of ours awakens and begins to move and shine. It begins to take on, again, the beauty that it had with the Father in the beginning. This is a thought-by-thought process; this is a word-by-word and act-by-act process. You don't just jump into this condition: You grow into it. You *work,* not giving thought to the negative, not emphasizing the patterns of destruction—the fear, the anger, the hate. You begin to move in the pattern that He has set. Turn the other cheek. Give the coat and the cloak also and walk the other mile. And we need to begin at home with those closest to us, for they present the most beautiful opportunities.

This is plain to thee. For as the law of sacrifice as committed unto men bespoke the coming of the law of mercy that was and is demonstrated in the life of the man Jesus, thy Christ, who offered Himself as a sacrifice once for all, entering into the holy of holies where He may meet thee day by day, thou art then indeed—as many as have named the name—come under the law of mercy, *not* of sacrifice.                    262-72

Let us pause a moment on that concept of sacrifice. You are aware of the great problem with sacrifice that man has faced down through the ages. There is hardly a religion of the world that hasn't sacrificed people as well as animals and products of the field. The stories of this are numerous. You can think of the one when Abraham climbed the mountain with the bundle of firewood which his son had collected. The son was to be the sacrifice. There were old altars in the Middle East into which the bodies of children were thrown, and some of these altars are still around. Ten thousand children, one after another, were sacrificed.

What in the name of high heaven was man in his history doing with a bunch of corn, asking a god of fertility to make more corn? Why was he sacrificing a goat for the gods to feast on? Remember the legends of Zeus. If a sacrifice wasn't burned in his honor, he'd throw a thunderbolt. If he liked the smell of the fires of the sacrifice, he'd send some rain for the crops. How did man get off in this direction? Let me suggest a way—and it ends with Jesus' final sacrifice. It has to do with the souls being trapped in matter, I think. Certainly, Edgar Cayce suggested that the projection of our spiritual being enmeshed us in matter. All around the world you can see pictures of pieces of human beings in trees. In Cambodia you can see these figures of men with chicken's feet and beaks on their faces. In many places there are pictures or sculptures of half-horses and half-man creatures; there are mermaids—all of these symbolizing man trapped in the earth, until he began to sacrifice the things that he was trapped in. He was going to destroy those and free the soul, so that it could reincarnate in a pure form and not be contaminated.

Man decided that he would free this spiritual soul, this being, by sacrificing—the fruit and, then, the animals and, finally, man himself. *Sacrifice*—to free us from the animal and allow a pure form to return. Now, of course, sacrifice is something that you and I have to do. It *is* necessary that we purify the body; but you and I ourselves are the ones who've got to do it. We can't impel others; we can't say to others, "You're an impure one, so you jump out of that body and come back in a pure form."

Jesus, I think, came to the end of this and used the cross as a way to demonstrate the release of the spirit. He pulled off the resurrection that man might know, without a doubt, that his spiritual being could purify itself. He reached that point. *Through His submitting, He overcame the very thing that was imposed upon Him.* The cross was the way to achieve the resurrection and to wipe out this idea of pressing upon others the notion of sacrifice. "That is not in the term that no man offers sacrifice, for the life of every soul that seeks in the material world to demonstrate the spiritual life is a life of sacrifice *from* the material angle. . ." (262-72)

We do have to learn, as He knew, to be able to give up that which blocks us in our spiritual movement and progression. We all know what we hold on to, the particular poison we use to tie us to the physical. We have to make that choice—and the choice is *ours,* not someone else's—so that we can begin to change and align ourselves with this pattern.

The reading continues:

. . .but to such that have passed from death unto life, in that law of mercy in naming Him as thine God, thine Brother, thine Savior, who has paid, who has offered Himself, thou art passed from death unto life—and the sacrifice is as *mercy* from thy God to thy brother. Hence he that would despitefully use thee, a kind word is as mercy. As ye would have mercy, show mercy. *Thou* knowest in thine heart.                   262-72

What a nice phrase—for "he that would despitefully use thee, a kind word is as mercy." It helps heal; it helps hold up the spiritual thrust that each of us is responsible for maintaining.

For it is line upon line, precept upon precept, here a little, there a little. Not some great deed then to show forth the love of the Father-God, but just being kind, just being patient, just being humble. These show forth in thy dealings with thy fellow man day by day that ye indeed walk, ye indeed talk, with thy Maker—who has promised to meet thee in the holy of holies within thine own self!

And as He, thy Brother, thy Savior has given, "Abide in me, and I will abide in thee; that the *glory* of the Father may be manifested to the children of men."                   1456-1

Hence these are as the greater openings for thyself. Think it not robbery to make thyself equal with God, for He is thy Father. Then approach Him in thy inner self as ye would thy earthly father. . .                   1581-2

As Jesus said, if you ask your heavenly Father for bread is He going to give you a stone? Is our heavenly Father any different from the one we have on earth? Is He not *more* just, *more* merciful? "Then approach Him in thy inner self as ye would thy earthly father, with that same conviction that He heareth and will answer thee—and that *thou* usest that understanding in thy relationship with thy fellow man!" (1581-2) In other words, if we're going to expect mercy and forgiveness from our Father in heaven, we need to forgive and to show mercy in simple ways in our relationship with this brother of ours that we're responsible for, beginning where we are and reaching out to him. "So when there are little jealousies, little hates, little selfishnesses, ye are hindering, ye are wounding the conscience, the love of the Father as manifests in thee. And His commandment is ever, 'Love one another.'" (1581-2)

Then be *thou* just to thy fellow man. For with what measure ye mete, for with what manner ye consider the lowliest of His children, is the mien with which ye wait on Him. Keep thy skirts *clean* from those things that make men—yea, that make the heart—doubt and fear. For the love of righteousness, of truth and mercy and judgment and justice, are the weapons with which ye may put *all things* to flight that would make thee afraid.                                    1580-1

There's a lot of fear that runs through all of us. What are the weapons that would put to flight those things that make us afraid? The love of righteousness, for one. What is righteousness? Right acts, as we know them, as we see them. Right acts toward our fellow man. Truth is another weapon. I must admit that, in my career, I am greatly stretched from time to time attempting to manifest this one. It is being honest, being truthful, being direct, expressing what you feel, what you believe, not giving half truths to people. It is rather shocking at times for people, but loving and living with truth, right acts—this is quite an operation. Lying is so much fun, and it's so easy. You think you can get what you want by lying, by pretending. Sometimes you don't even have to say anything. You can just *be* a lie.

Mercy is a weapon, being merciful. Judgment is another. What in the world is judgment doing here? We thought we were getting rid of judging. Why are you and I most judged inside ourselves? We must be willing to measure up against the ideals and purposes we have set, be willing to bring our thoughts and our words and our acts before this measure that we set as the pattern, as the ideal, as the principle for our life. That's the judgment I think the reading is talking about here: the willingness to face ourselves, the willingness to measure against ideals and purposes, every word, every thought, and every act of our lives. And finally, justice—this is to oneself and to others. Fairness, not only with others, but with self. Be fair.

And it is thus that He stands, not as a Lord but as thy Brother, as thy Savior; that ye may know indeed the truth that gentleness, kindness, patience, brotherly love, beget—in thy heart of hearts, with Him—that peace, that harmony. Not as the world knoweth peace but as He gave: "That peace I give you; that ye may know that thy spirit, yea thy soul, beareth witness with me that ye are mine—and I am thine," even as the Father, the Son, the Holy Spirit.

Even so may thy soul, thy mind, thy body, become aware of that which renews the hope, the faith, the patience within thee. 987-4

"What is the Godhead? Father, Son and Holy Spirit." (3188-1)

Now here is a phrase that we must all consider carefully: "There is the outpouring of the spirit on thee as ye pour it out upon thy fellow man." (3188-1) Now what is this Spirit we're talking about, this spiritual energy, this one force? Man has begun to fumble a bit with this idea. Man has come to know that love—physical love—is a matter of mutual giving: As one gives, one receives, and, without this, there is no expression in reality. Even at the physical level of expression, there must be the give and the take, the sharing, the outpouring; without it, without "the outpouring. . .on thee," there can be no relationship, no genuine relationship.

It is impossible to have peace in our lives until we are willing to begin to bring peace rather than tension into the lives of those we meet day by day. Man—the flesh, the animal man, the body that we created, the thought form that we builded—is filled with the violence in the history of man, and we've come to love violence, even in small ways. We scream at each other to let out this energy. Yet we must, if we are to bring peace into the earth, become a channel for peace and quietness flowing through us in our thoughts, first, and, then, in our words and in our lives. This is the spirit, the energy, the soul quality of man, directed deliberately by us, so that the Spirit of God may be awakened in others. This is our responsibility as our brother's keeper.

We are so easily caught up in the small contentions and fumings and worry and bickering in our lives—in the things that do not really matter most of the time and tomorrow will be gone. But for the moment, we love the excitement and the screaming and the hollering and the tumult and the fury in small things. I'm not talking about the wars in which man engages himself. I'm talking about the small, everyday life energies and activities. At these times, we must sense our relationship to our brother and become a channel for this energy moving at a spiritual level, rather than being used for contention. We are our brother's keeper in this sense. "There is the outpouring of the spirit on thee as ye pour it out upon thy fellow man. For, as ye do it unto the least of thy brethren, ye do it unto thy Maker." (3188-1)

You may remember that I've spent a little time in church activities. When we first begin to read the Bible and think about Jesus, His healing is so far beyond our abilities that it seems impossible that He could have meant it when He said, "Go and do likewise." Let's think about this business of healing in relationship to our fellow man. It needs much thought and development and work on your part, and mine, in dealing with the memories that others have about us and our responsibility in relationship to those.

It's my opinion that these Edgar Cayce readings suggest that you and I, whether we like it or not, either pull down or heal every single individual we touch throughout our lives. There is no middle ground here. We do this in a multitude of ways. Our thought patterns, our anger, our irritation, our annoyance stimulate that thought form that exists within another person. These things may not even be related to us. They may just be negative hate or anger or fear; but we turn it on, increase it, as we come in contact with others. Words and actions do exactly the same thing, and we hurt, pull down, drain, or stir the negative in every single soul we touch. The more sensitive and more aware we become, the more active this is. It reaches a point where we even begin to be aware of doing this; and, at that point, if we either unconsciously or consciously misuse that power, we suffer for it through natural law.

We are all healers, and so we are responsible. Now, we can go too far and depend only on ourselves; but when we turn around and become a channel through which *God,* the spiritual energy, flows naturally, then, the effect is true healing through such simple means as thought, word, prayer, or the touch of the hand.

As we read the Bible, we think of Jesus, of all His physical healings. There were differences in those healings: I'm sure that Matthew, the tax collector, was healed in a different manner than Zaccheus, who had so much money, whom everybody in the city owed, who was up in the tree trying to see

Jesus. Jesus said, "I'm coming to have dinner with you today." And Zaccheus gave back all the money he'd been stealing from people. That's a healing of a different kind.

You have to read the descriptions of Jesus' life to realize that every moment of His experience was an outpouring of the spiritual energy to everyone He touched, and He healed them all again and again and again. You and I must realize this responsibility. We must be aware of the need to so align our bodies and our minds that our love and our concern and our caring can begin to be a healing influence in the lives of every person with whom we associate—not contention, not irritation, not screaming.

You say, "But they are such so-and-sos!" Jesus didn't say they weren't. He just said what *you* need to do and be. We must be prepared to be a channel of healing for all those who touch our lives, physically, emotionally, spiritually, and on all the levels of concern. We must be aware of these things or we will destroy, we will hurt—and we will suffer as a result, by the natural law of cause and effect.

It is God's love, God's grace, that He would have go through our lives to the degree that we can achieve this. You say, "Well, I've tried it and it gets to be pretty hairy." Yes, it does. It's as if you set a light in the window and throw the door open and you don't know who's coming through at any minute. The opportunities are multitudinous. But it is impossible to attract anything that you cannot deal with if you are lined up with God and this pattern that Jesus has set down for us in His admonitions, in the demonstration of His life. It may take, at times, a little extra prayer and fasting. He spoke about that under the difficut times and places, you remember. It may take more work on our part, and we may grow tired, but there is renewal in this alignment and in this becoming a channel, rather than taking an ego trip on our own.

Pray for each other. Healing comes at all the levels of the body and the mind and the emotions. It can be as simple as suggesting a castor oil pack at the right time, or praying for somebody, or listening to them when they need to be listened to. That, too, is healing and loving, at all the levels of healing. We are charged by the Christ pattern to go and do likewise. And there are people close to us with whom and for whom we can be the very best channel of healing for obvious reasons.

"Then, turn to thine own opportunity within to know Him while it is yet day in thine own material consciousness." (1759-1) What is this "while it is yet day"? In all of our lives there come the dark times. It is in these daylight periods, when we are aware, when we are thinking positively, when we are praying and we're working, that we can make the alignment and set the goals so that in those dark periods when we can't see so well, when we stumble, there will be some light to follow.

"Sow the seeds of truth, of brotherly love, of kindness, of gentleness, of patience. And know, that alone ye possess is that which ye have *given away!*" (1759-1) You've heard this many times. Edgar Cayce paraphrases it here: Only that which we can give away is really ours.

That which ye command or demand is never a defense, but rather a judgment ye have set upon thine own self.

Then, let thy well [wellspring?] be renewed within thee, that ye may show forth in the days of thy awareness as to thy relationship to thy brother, that ye take thought of him, in that as ye would have men do to you, ye do even so to them.

For this experience is for thy own holiness, if ye will but look to Him. For God hath not willed that any soul should be in shame, in discouragement, bound with the fetters of circumstance or of obligation, but would have thee *free*—as He hath given thee thine *own* will—yea, thine own soul, and said "If ye will be my son, I will be thy God."

Hast thou drawn away? Hast thou neglected thy sonship, thy kinship with thy Maker?                                    1759-1

"Count it rather as an opportunity, a gift of a merciful Father, that there *are* the opportunities in the present for the sojourn in the material influences. . .count thy friends as the greatest of thy opportunities." (1709-3) Every kid (I don't know much about girls growing up, but certainly little boys growing up) reaches a period in adolescence where friendship is love in a blood sense: They do things with their wrists and make pacts. Great comradeship exists at that period. Friendship is but a symbol of the love, the awakening of this divine, creative energy that bubbles up, and some of the greatest essays of man have been written about it.

". . .count thy friends as the greatest of thy opportunities." (1709-3) Most of us are very, very cautious about friends as we grow older. We've learned they can hurt us. Only the people you love can hurt you; you know that. Love is an investment, and we become afraid to invest ourselves in love. Now and then, though, despite ourselves, we draw near to it and it begins to flow. It's a beautiful thing, the joyous freedom of it in expression. Don't be afraid to invest in friends.

"Since every act of love becomes in its application not rote, but a renewing, a regeneration, a growth, thus does it become as He gave from that experience, 'To him that betook of that which to him was unholy partake no more. Let him that had spoken unkindly, speak unkindly no more. Let him that had failed in showing forth love, fail no more.'" These are very specific, very concrete, very applicable at a very simple, daily level in our lives as we face the responsibility of being our brother's keeper.

"To him that betook [and he's speaking to us] of that which to him [to *him*—not to somebody else] was unholy partake no more. Let him that had spoken unkindly, speak unkindly no more. Let him that had failed in showing forth love, fail no more." And this includes every single one of us; you know it and I know it.

"Let that rather be thy watchword, 'I am my brother's keeper.'" (2780-3)

Let us be about our Father's business.

# Jesus' Concept of the Father

From the Edgar Cayce readings' perspective, what did Jesus think about His Father? When we come to this concept of Jesus, we discover, of course, that He said, "I and my Father are one." The oneness is established there.

It is important for us not to just get caught up in the words but, having read the words, begin to back up and try to understand them through experiencing their meaning. Intellectually, we can build barriers to an understanding of these concepts. So, instead, try to look toward experiencing the oneness of God, and not just intellectually grasping it. It is possible for you and me to experience oneness—not intellectually but in the movement of consciousness.

First, we will build these concepts from the readings, and then you're going to need to work with them in your meditations, in your dream experiences, in your relations with one another, in your groups, in your families, and with the people you work with and pray for and who pray for you, because you will begin, then, to sense this oneness of experience. In a way, what's going to happen to you is that you're going to fall in love with everybody—even the ones who really are a little too much for you. That's what it's all about.

"'Know, O Israel, the Lord thy God is one.' All power, all force, is a manifestation of that which is termed God consciousness." "Know, O Israel, the Lord thy God is one." This quote runs throughout these readings, and surely Jesus talked again and again about this oneness with His Father.

The concept of the oneness of all force is a difficult one to get a grasp on. The first principle of oneness we need to work with is this: our mental, physical and spiritual bodies are all one. We've got strange attitudes about our bodies and about ourselves. It's hard for us to believe that this body that we think has caused us so much trouble is one with our mental and spiritual bodies. We think of the flesh body as a weak and lowly thing, desiring everything that has gotten us into so much trouble. We think that just as soon as we can get out of it and take off into the universe everything will be fine. Nothing could be further from the truth! You and I are going to be around until we get this body straightened out. There isn't any use talking about going anywhere until then.

The real physical body, however, is one that is vibrating a little faster than this flesh body, but it is still atomic in its structure. It is the one which has the out-of-body experiences, the one we inhabit as soon as we die. It is physical and is involved in all of those desires. It is the one that has gotten us involved in matter and is the one—the part of us—that suffers a bit now. This body must be seen as a part of the whole. The physical body, the mental body, and the spiritual body are all one.

"Know, O Israel, the Lord thy God is one." Now, let's discuss a major issue that's in our minds—the concept of the devil. How can God be one if there is a devil abroad in the earth, chasing after us, working, appearing and doing all these despicable things that get us into so much trouble? You know, the devil really has got a publicity man working. When he sold comedian Flip Wilson that little phrase, "The devil made me do it," he got himself in front of more people. "Geraldine" (Flip) has said, "The devil made me do it," lots of times and said it most effectively. You and I have said it many times, and we keep on saying it. Sometimes it's the devil in somebody else. Sometimes it's the devil in our society. Sometimes it's the devil in our families. Sometimes we hang it on the Russians or anybody else that happens to be convenient.

The devil. Now, what is this concept? If you study the Cayce readings carefully, you will learn that the devil is defined as rebellion. You and I see it, I suspect, as the dark side of ourselves, the dark side of humanity.

There's not a one of us who does not dream repeatedly of a symbol that pulls us back, that strives to defeat us. It represents the feeding of those desire patterns of our body's thought forms. Some of us may use animals or some despicable-looking characters. Some of us use the symbols of our neighbors whom we dislike. We dream, not of them but of ourselves and the negative in ourselves. So the devil, in a sense, works through those.

From the readings' point of view, did God create a devil? Yes, but it was a part of the oneness of all force. There was a rebellion. You and I became a part of that rebellion and departed from God consciousness. However, we are God created, not self-created. It is God—not we—who created us and, in this sense, we are part of this whole.

The readings speak of angelic beings, of advanced souls, who slip in and try to help. (You may choose to see them as purely symbolic.) We hang all sorts of designations on them from time to time, but in the original creation they were a part of the creative power and the oneness. There is but *one* force. What we do with it—how we use this creative energy that we are custodians of and how we move to express it—is our choice.

The will was part of the original essence of the soul itself: the divine mind, the divine will, a part of the divine spirit or energy or life force, so that we have choice. We can align ourselves with all that represents rebellion in the earth, or we can align ourselves with all that represents the lighted path and the return to God consciousness, which is patterned in Jesus the Christ.

Let's bring this consciousness down and not leave it with the rebellious angels, like Satan, or the rebellious souls. I have often thought that both Jesus' movement down into consciousness and angels' leading of the souls away from God consciousness became a symbol of the devil. "I am the vine and ye are the branches." When He turned over a new leaf, as the expression goes, and started back, He became the Christ. Think about that. It's an interesting idea.

Let me show you why it's so interesting. You and I do this all the time in our lives. We have a variety of energies, but we use just one energy. There aren't two or three or four or five different kinds of energy, but one energy. We direct it in different ways in our experience at any level of consciousness.

When you get angry, you build thought patterns. You create thought forms. You exude energy, which actually flows out of you from the adrenal gland center like a pump. It blasts people. This drive, used negatively, is still the one energy; it is not something different. This is a very difficult concept to understand and to separate in our consciousness. Courage is that same energy flowing positively as is the drive to get things done and to accomplish something.

Self-pity might be located at the thymus level. Every time someone begins to complain about the world, other people or themselves, they blast this energy and use it destructively. They tear apart—literally—the physical parts of the body. It is the same energy that is used in sex, which we have arranged in a variety of ways, have so much fun with, and get so hung up on at times. It is also the expression of creation: a beautiful poem or painting or music. Or hate. Or healing prayer. All of this is one energy directed by mankind.

So, when you read, "Know, O Israel, the Lord thy God is one," realize that what is being said is that, as we use this one energy, we declare unto the world the way we look at our God. The way we worship our God, what we think of this creative power of the universe, how we relate to it, are not all mouthed in words but expressed in our lives, as we direct these energies constructively or destructively according to our choice.

There isn't any way we're going to avoid facing this. This is where we live, where we are. So we need to begin to understand and relate to this concept of oneness. It is God's energy, God's being, that we use. It is God's completeness—not ourselves—that we direct in every thought, every word and every act of our lives.

Jesus said, "...the Father that dwelleth in me, He doeth the works." Nothing that I do has meaning in this sense of the concept of God's oneness. We must remember who we are and why we're here and what we've got to do in the earth. We are His and we must act like it!

Now, let's look at another reading:

In the Godhead there is found still the three-dimensional concept—God the Father, God the Son, and God the Holy Spirit.

Hence—if this is acceptable to the entity in its conception of that which has been, which is, which may be—these are still founded in that summed up in "The Lord thy God is one."

Also, in the interpretation of the universe, we find that time and space are concepts of the mental mind, as to an interpretation of or a study into the relationships with man and to the universal or God consciousness.        1747-5

Another reading stated:

So man's concept of the Godhead is three-dimensional—Father, Son and Holy Spirit. The communication or the activity or the motivating force we find is three-dimensional—time, space and patience. Neither of these exists in fact, except in the concept of the individual as it may apply to time or space or patience.        4035-1

What does this mean? There is no time except in the mind. There is no space except in the mind. We avoid facing this until we begin to dream, until we begin to move in meditation, until our bodies become sensitive enough and tuned enough to be able to experience it. There is no time or space except in the mind. It's all one in patience. This is a concept that needs to be experienced. It is something that cannot be grasped just intellectually.

Several items can be used to illustrate measures of time: a notched stick, an hourglass, a sun dial. There's even a complicated hand piece with a sweep hand which measures every second, based on the disintegration of a particular kind of atomic structure. That's what we're measuring time by, these days. We used to measure it by the stars.

But there isn't any reality to time and space. This is the first barrier to our understanding and, at the same time, the first way in which we begin to sense this truth. In psychic activities, such as precognition or clairvoyance, we have experiences that transcend time and space. How can you measure space when a man, lying in a sunlit room here in Virginia Beach, describes something a thousand miles away—with absolute accuracy? What has time and space got to do with that kind of perception? How is it possible? How can an electroencephalogram work on a man in Moscow when a man in Leningrad is *thinking* a word to put him to sleep? There is no time lapse at that moment between Moscow and Leningrad when that thought registers and when his brain pattern begins to change. This experiment has been repeated again and again. How can you conceive of time and space in these kinds of experiences? How can you dream and know you were in two places at once? Two times? Two incarnations at once? Two experiences in the earth? It's simple to illustrate, but very hard to experience.

I could put my hand on a book and feel the book in five places at once. Why can't I experience five lives at once? Because I am so bogged down here in one life that I can't move to this consciousness to experience the oneness, the oneness of experience. All of our lives are going on at *one time*—not separately, not in any sort of order. They're not as if on a ladder, but they are spread out in the universe.

We are citizens of this universe, as we begin to move to a God consciousness. Surely Jesus said this and, better still, demonstrated it. He never touched a person with His mind or with His body that He didn't lift them, that He didn't heal them. He demonstrated this oneness, this constant, continuous flow of spiritual energy. You and I should go and do likewise, even if it takes the hide off of us. And sometimes it does! Yet we can come to love, to relate, understand and apply the law of love. It can be done.

"For remember, the Father God hath promised to meet thee in

thy temple." The temple is the body. Now we've got to get that body in shape for Him to meet us there. If it's out of kilter, out of shape, it's very difficult for us to make the connection, to turn the right knobs to get the right picture, like a TV set or radio being tuned to cut out the static. The static is what we've built up—our thought forms, the condition of our bodies.

Remember, this body changes so quickly that if you don't like what you are now, you can change it. Tomorrow you can make a different one. You've got billions of cells that you're working on every day. So, the change is in process now at the flesh level.

But the temple the reading is talking about here, I think, constitutes both the flesh body and the real physical body—the finer body that is moving so fast we can't see it, but it interpenetrates the whole. It's the one that is affected by healing so much quicker than the flesh body and the one in which we move in out-of-body experiences, the one we use when we get rid of this flesh.

"For remember, the Father God hath promised to meet thee in thy temple." The importance of the body in the readings is without question. Why did Jesus do so much work in healing? Why did Cayce give nearly 9,000 readings on healing alone? The flesh body that contains the real physical body is so important in its balancing, in its attunement, in order to make possible this meeting with God within, in prayer, in meditation.

It's the body that so frequently blocks us in our meditation and prayer experiences. We need to tune it up, to cleanse it, to balance it, to discipline it. Discipline is a harsh word for some, but all it takes is just pulling your hand back when you reach out, pulling it back before it gets there. Watch yourself as you go through a cafeteria line and you'll discover how much you're exercising discipline.

So this body, then, is part of this whole, this oneness. "Thy body is as the shadow of the tabernacle, and He will meet thee in the holy of holies. Remember as thy Master, thy Lord, the Christ, has given, 'I stand at the door and knock. If you open, I will enter and abide with thee.'"

Jesus is broadcasting all the time, but we don't tune in to it. We don't adjust our sets because we haven't always got what it takes to make this attunement possible.

This is what it's about. This is the way we can begin to understand the Father whom Jesus was talking about, the Father He was representing and that He insisted that you and I also represent. That's a great challenge, but it is also a great responsibility and a great opportunity to fulfill that kind of promise. What else have you got to do here this time that really matters?

### Then how do they apply in thyself?

As ye have been taught, as ye are aware, the Godhead is the Father, the Son, the Holy Spirit. Just as in thyself—as the pattern—the body, the mind, the soul. They are one, just as the Father, the Son, the Holy Spirit are one. They each functioning in coordination or cooperation as one with another become as thy own experiences in a material world, the awareness of the consciousness of that God-force, that Spirit abiding within.

Then, there has been given, there has been shown the way that the Father is mindful of His children; that these as they appear in the earth—yea, thyself—are a portion of His manifestation. Not as an indefinite force, not as an unconcrete thing, not as just a mist, but just as is manifested not only in the Christ but as is manifested in thee—thy desires to do right, thy desires that there be the manifesting of love, of patience, of hope, of long-suffering, of brotherly kindness, of doing good even when others speak unkindly, when others revile thee, when others say those things that in thy physical consciousness find resentment.

But as He manifests—as a portion of that Godhead that is represented in thee, as *in* thy mind—then ye become aware that ye are *indeed* a child of the living God, and are in materiality for those purposes of manifesting those very things that are the fruits of the Spirit in thy dealings with thy fellow man.                    1348-1

The body is indeed the temple of the living God. All of God, then, that you may know is manifested in and through yourself—not what somebody else thinks or what somebody else does, for that is the nice way of the devil and his workshop: to do, because somebody else does, or think a certain way just because somebody else does.

This realization, this movement in consciousness, these steps that we need to take in aligning ourselves are done through the expression of the fruits of the Spirit: love, patience, kindness, and long-suffering. As we move to be still, to quicken and to cleanse, we move toward God consciousness. It is within.

This is not a pantheistic concept of a dispersal of energy without any consciousness. It is a soul awareness, a soul created as a special kind of energy pattern of which we are a part. We each have a job to do here in the earth.

This God we've been looking at, this concept of the Father, is a creator. Yes, a creator of all, of everything. A loving Father?

Obviously. Caring, reaching out, with grace constantly flowing and available to us? Part of each of us? Yes. We're part of this whole. I think this is the God about whom Jesus spoke. A loving father, a creator, one that He was in and part of, one in whom everything that was done was done through Him. He did nothing of Himself. Without that God moving through Him He would—could—have done nothing. Yet it is challenging to us that we could be one with this whole in awareness and consciousness. This is the Father who, I think, appears in these readings, the Father about whom Jesus spoke.

# Jesus' Teaching on Meditation

Years ago, I knew a man by the name of Tom Sugrue. As you may know, he wrote the biography of Edgar Cayce, *There Is a River.* Tom came from Naugatuck, Connecticut, and I came to know Naugatuck through Tom's mind and through his writing, as if I had lived there. Tom was Catholic, and we fought all through college about psychical research.

He began to write and dream about the kind of church that he hoped the Catholic Church would become. From his book, *Stranger in the Earth,* I would share with you a passage that I often use to close a lecture.

This is Tom Sugrue's description of a church he dreamed of on the Naugatuck Green. (I think in a thought world it is really there.) "Any man could enter the church and ask for a priest or a priestess and speak with him or with her of the things that troubled him. In a small, quiet room, with light streaming from a skylight and books on a table, he sat and talked, telling what lay in his heart: [All of us have been at this point, I think.] 'I know not who I am, nor whence I came, nor what I am here to perform. This is a dark place, full of fears and shouting. The land gives me sustenance and they who are my fellows take it from me. I hear there is a God, locked up in a thousand churches. I am told there is a devil, loose in the fields and in the streets. I am condemned because my body takes heat and seeks to warm with it the womb of a woman. What is my sin and who shall punish it? Am I a name in a book or a tree without roots or a thought which God has cast out to the land of rejection, where things which come imperfect from the mold are scattered and left to decay?'

"The priest or priestess [answers]: 'We read shadows which are made by the passing of light. What seems true is only the reflection of truth, thrown from a hundred thousand suns, flickering briefly on the dark wall of our world. What we know is what the mind knows and what the heart feels. The mind is an edge of another mind, from which it is cut off. It is shut up, sealed out, and blinded. It can only listen as the mind from which it is cut off goes by, and try to remember what that mind is like. The heart is the edge of another heart, from which it is cut off. It is shut up, sealed out, and blinded. It can only listen as it beats to the beat of the heart from which it is cut off, and try to recall the rhythm and the music from which that faraway ecstasy is made. You are a mind and a heart cut off. This is what we know about you.

"'The great mind is the mind of God, to which your mind must return, and the great heart is the heart of God, to which your heart must return. Then your thoughts will know the thoughts of all creation, and your heart will beat with the heart of God.

"'But now, you are alone, sent on a long adventure, to help God bring creation to its flower. You are His agent, bearing His love. Your heart hears faintly His song. Make yourself a part of that song, that those who have lost that tune may find it. Consider not whether you are fed or clothed or housed, but only whether you love and pray and serve. When you work, think of God. When you rest, let Him hold you. When you reach out, touch His hand, and then put your arm around a friend.'"
(*Stranger in the Earth,* pp. 113-114)

That is where you and I are.

That is the Edgar Cayce readings summed up, put together in a simple philosophical statement. The Man who has shown the way—the part of God who has shown the way along this path that you and I are walking—is the man we will discuss. We will talk about Him from many different directions and in many different ways. I will try to point you to places in the Edgar Cayce readings that for me have shown some light, some insight. I will try to share with you experiences that I have had trying to struggle along this path, for you and I are charged with a great responsibility. There is not a person who is not responsible for some other people and who, through those, eventually touches hundreds of people. We have a model. We have a way. We have a light. And you and I know now that this is not a dark and dismal walk that we must suffer alone but a lighted path that we can follow. And we had best be about our Father's business.

I knew another man—his name was Edgar Cayce—and he was one of the most disturbed, most confused men I have ever known—and one of the most beautiful. He had a capacity to love and care about people such as I have never seen since in this life. He began, as you know, unable to function, unable to talk, caught up in physical disabilities—bewildered—and then discovered that (out of his own unconscious, by tuning within) he could somehow tap a source of the higher self that could give him directions for healing. The instructions were followed, and he was healed. For 43 years, he said repeatedly, "This you can do also. It is easy to make this connection." He said over and over again that the way to achieve this is by following the lighted path that has been walked for us—and he began to describe it.

At the time of those early readings, he didn't know what to do with the power he had. He was confused by it. He had been in Sunday school all of his life. He taught Sunday school; he worked with the Bible constantly all of his life. Then, he was confronted with my mother who was dying with tuberculosis. Through the readings, he gave information that saved her. When he tried to use this ability in a kind of business with doctors (he worked as a photographer and also gave readings), people began to misuse him and he got sick. He then ran away, gave it all up, stopped giving readings. Nobody knew where he was. He ended up in Selma, Alabama, in a photographic shop. People found him, though, saying, "Go to sleep and talk about me."

Around that time, I burned my eyes with flash powder in an accident. He had to save my eyesight, and it helped bring him to a realization. By 1923, he had committed himself to doing nothing but the readings, giving up the business and throwing away what he had achieved as a photographer. He starved, literally starved. I came from school in Selma to that house in Dayton, Ohio (where he had moved the family), merely to satisfy the four people who were there. But after the meal that day, he handed me a nine-page document called a life reading. This started something. The philosophy of the readings opened up in 1923. And the dream readings began and out of them poured something which did not just challenge to gargle with Glyco-Thymoline or slap on castor oil packs or eat properly and quit smoking (which he didn't do, by the way) and do all kinds of things to balance the flesh we have to work through: The readings began to deal with *concepts*. They dealt with karma and grace and, from a historical point of view, began to talk about our dreams as an access, as a way. They began to talk about setting ideals. They began to talk about meditation and to recommend it.

Edgar Cayce began to come forth with the most fantastic, crazy concept related to this Bible that he loved, that he worked with, that he could make come alive. I watched him with the largest Sunday school classes in the state of Alabama. I watched him with little juniors who became Christian Endeavor experts. I watched him make the Bible come alive for hundreds and hundreds of people—children and adults—all over this country. And out of these readings came these strange ideas regarding Jesus who became the Christ. He phrased it that way. And he began to put together, for me, some ideas that are not just theories, but concepts that we can take and work with in our own lives—for this is where the difference lies. The philosophy in the Edgar Cayce readings—make no mistake about it—is not theory. It is workable, usable concepts and ideas which you and I are challenged to try, to work with, and then deal with the results.

We're not to automatically believe all this just because it came out of an unconscious mind. If you believe everything that comes out of unconscious minds—yours or other people's—you are in for a *strange* trip that will be worse than any LSD trip or drug trip you ever took or ever saw anybody take. What we must do is to take the ideas and test them. In some way, we must take the information from the Edgar Cayce readings that deal with Jesus who became the Christ and put it into a workable, usable ideal—a path, a way which we can follow. And I think we can. Mine is an individual interpretation. This is what I have found and what I have tried to use, but you can't take it and say, "Yes, that's fine." You've got to deal with it and wrestle with it and work with it yourself and put it into your life and then talk about *your* results, not mine. This is just my point of view. I will lay it down; you have to pick it up. It's not going to jump on you or jump down your throat or wrap around you somehow and mystically and magically change you. I might move you with words, but the excitement of the moment is easily lost. You have to reach out and take it and work with it *persistently*. But I can say that, for me, this is the most exciting, the most challenging material in all of the Edgar Cayce readings. And, for me, it has worked!

In the past three months, I have been away from A.R.E. I've been writing and I've been gardening. I've been trying to get a nature spirit to work and I've discovered he only works when I work. But I have doubled in that time—and tripled—my prayer and meditation. And I have had the most beautiful meditation experiences and the most beautiful prayer experiences, and the most beautiful results, that I have ever had in all my life. I will try in a way to share some of these with you.

It is easy to become confused. You and I are living in a

strange world, a world of illusion. It is a world that we see so dimly. We are working through five senses—none of which gives us a picture of what is really going on. There are very few of us with the ability to clearly see the television shows that are running through the atmosphere around us. Or to hear all of the music from the dozens of radio stations that are also there. Why can't we? We know they are present. We can take a couple of little boxes and turn them on and see and hear. Why can't we hear and see without them? Someone you know may have a problem that you have solved, that you have worked with, that you know how to help—but you don't even know they have the problem. You are not aware of what the need is. You have talents; you have abilities; you know how to pray for people; you've gotten results. Someone close to you may need what you have. Why can't we stop long enough to sense, to know, to reach out, to touch, to pray, even to smile and share?

What is it that has blinded man? How did we get this way? How did we become confused? In talking about this subject the other night, I told some stories. They are old ones, but they are clear illustrations: A little boy went to the hospital to have his tonsils taken out. He was just a little boy, hadn't started to school. His mother was with him. She stopped by around supper time, and she said to the nurse in the hall, "Johnny's in there by himself. I've got to run home and give supper to the other children. I'm coming right back. Will you just step in there and check on him every so often and see that he is all right? He is a very frightened little boy and he's going to have his tonsils out tomorrow."

The nurse said, "Certainly, I'll take care of it." Johnny was all by himself there in his room, and the nurse, being in a very modern hospital, picked up the intercom. Out of the wall right up there above Johnny's bed came this voice, "How are you, Johnny? Your mother's gone to give supper to the other children. She'll be right back. How are you?" Not a sound in reply. "Johnny, Johnny, I know you're there. Now answer me," she said.

And over the intercom, coming back, was this frightened little voice: "What do you want, Wall?"

One I like even more is much older: we all feel this way at times. A little boy was praying. (His mother had told him that he should pray each night. She had said, "Now, Bobby, God watches you all the time, and you must pray every night.") And so, that night she stopped by, and he was on his knees praying for everybody—including the cat and the dog. At the end, as she

stood listening, she heard him say in an odd little voice, "God...
God. . .I know you're there. But if you move, you're going to
scare me to death!"

You and I are like this. As you work and search along this
path, remember always that there are two points of view: yours
and someone else's—and the right one. This is well illustrated
in another old story: A man was out hunting bears and he shot
at a bear. He didn't kill him, but he made him mad. The man
began to run, and the bear was running right after him. The
man ran up a canyon, and the canyon began to get narrower
and narrower. As he got to the end of the canyon and realized he
couldn't climb out of this thing, he could hear the bear coming
after him. In great desperation he dropped down on his knees,
crying, "God, save me from this monster!" And there wasn't a
sound. He heard the bear still coming and then he heard a
crunch. He opened his eyes and was amazed to see the bear with
his paws up saying, "God, I thank you for the wonderful meal
you have provided for me." There are always two points of view.
Remember that.

We have to talk about the fall of man in order to understand
Jesus. I'm not going to discuss this in depth. You can read about
this in Eula Allen's beautiful books, *The Creation Trilogy*,
which contain some interesting and strange ideas, some very
peculiar concepts from the readings regarding man's history.
You and I, as spiritual beings, pushed down into the earth
plane. Most of you are familiar with this. You wrestle with it,
you kick it around, you realize gradually that if you've been in
and out of the earth many times that life is going on, not here
alone, but in other planes of consciousness simultaneously.
This is quite a journey.

We must grasp and work with this concept that the man we
know as Jesus walked this way and, as He walked, lighted the
path that He walked. Now, as the readings suggest, he didn't
walk it just as Jesus, but appeared at other times and places.
For example, the Edgar Cayce readings suggest that He
showed up as Zend. Unless you were a good Zoroastrian
somewhere down the line, you'll probably never read the Zend-
Avesta. It comes out of Persia, and when Jesus was a little boy,
He went back to Persia, according to Edgar Cayce, and sort of
reviewed some of the teachings that He had Himself started
when He was there earlier.

According to the readings, He went to India and He went to
Egypt. This blew everybody's mind, including my father's—
who had great difficulty accepting the tremendous dimensions

of the world history view and the concept that Jesus moved in and out of the earth.

I want to look at a Bible passage here. In the readings, as I understand them, there is a suggestion that Jesus was responsible. That soul we know, that part of God who was the first begotten of the Father was responsible for the coming of other souls. We followed Him into the earth, and we have His strange statement in Luke 10:17-20: "And the seventy returned again with joy, saying, Lord, even the devils are subject unto us through thy name. [In other words, "We could do anything; we could heal anybody."] And He said unto them, I beheld Satan as lightning fall from heaven. Behold, I give unto you power to tread on serpents and scorpions, and over all the power of the enemy: and nothing shall by any means hurt you. Notwithstanding in this rejoice not, that the spirits are subject unto you; but rather rejoice, because your names are written in heaven."

I think there is a whole cycle of souls in the earth who are party to this. He is speaking to *us*. Now, He found some He could put to work right then, 2,000 years ago when He was here, but He keeps trying to put us to work now—and through us— work to bring about a total healing. Think of that Satan when He came down. If you turn that coin over, it is the Savior that came down, and there isn't but one in that sense. Yes, I am saying He is one and the same, as I understand it. That is the most beautiful way I have found to get rid of the devil, to put him in the place where he belongs. He's in the rebellious part of us. He's there when we break the law, when we rebel, when we— in our egos, in our drive—*fail* to do: fail to heal where we can heal, pray where we should be praying, touch where we should be touching, smile where we should be smiling and helping.

Edgar Cayce gave Jesus an incarnation as Melchizedek. That was an interesting gentleman who lived in a place of peace called Salem. Abraham, who had been chasing some robbers who had stolen his cattle, caught them, got his cattle back, killed all the people—and stoppped back by Salem. He paid some tithes to Melchizedek, then drank wine and broke bread with this prince of peace. (It is a strange picture that emerges of a universal Christ!)

The readings infer that Jesus was in Egypt as Hermes. Other lifetimes in many places were also given. They trace Him particularly in the Jewish tradition. Of Amilius. Edgar Cayce gave that name for the first projection in the earth. In Adam and others. And so, we come to this man we know, we call,

Jesus. Back of Him are many lives. In many times and places He walked the path here.

What did He lay down? What are the basic principles that we must be very aware of as we begin to work with Him? The first is very simple—but if you remember nothing else I say, remember this: *Jesus never claimed to do anything of Himself.* "It is the Father that worketh in and through me. I and the Father are one. He is in me; I'm in you," He said in talking day by day with the people whom He worked with there. But He speaks to us in the same way. And what He is saying is that you and I must let go of this ego. There is nothing so dangerous as spiritual egotism, nothing so deadly and dangerous. *"I healed . . .I. . .I. . .I."* This ego is not where it's at. We must find, as He said, this kingdom of heaven within—within us.

The dependence, then, on the God within is this first direction. We must also recognize that as He moved along this path and showed, as He taught the seventy to go out and heal, to go out and serve and work, so He has provided us the miracles. The miracles, from Edgar Cayce's point of view, were real. They were not some magic; they were not some psychological twist. You've read those Bible criticisms today that even argue about the existence of Jesus, and they try to get rid of the miracles of Jesus—such as when He fed the 5,000. (Everybody had brought a lunch but they had it tucked away. And He shamed them into sharing it with each other and they all got their lunches out and shared them.) Well, it's hard for us to realize, to perceive, that there can, indeed, be multiplication, that the silver and the gold and the cattle on a thousand hills belong to the Lord of this universe and there is plenty.

We are so used to being unable to perceive, to see, to hear. We just mentioned that we cannot see the television all around us or hear the radio music that plays, much less the celestial music that is available at higher levels of consciousness. And so it is hard for us to grasp that these miracles are possible for us. I've seen them. You've seen them, too, in little things and little ways. You've seen them in your groups where there was prayer and there was healing. You've seen them in the lives of children that you loved and prayed for. You've seen them with friends that you reached out to. Not by what you said, but by what you did, the creative energy that moved through you as you made yourself a channel healed and changed.

Yesterday I was with a young man whom I have seen change and become creative. Coming from destruction and condemnation and criticism and a violence you wouldn't believe in a young person unless you'd seen it, he has become balanced, normal, creative. Painting, writing, sculpturing burst out of him, and he is playing a part in the vast drama that we are all very much involved in, a part that may quicken the consciousness of men all over this world. He is playing a part in the reality of this new age, and it is simply because people loved him enough and cared enough to help him take some steps along this path. You don't know what you are dealing with in your children, in your friends. You don't know the infinite capacity for creative accomplishment that is locked inside each and every one of us. This is what Jesus is saying to us. Make that contact with Him yourself, and you can be, indeed, God's agent in the earth.

The resurrection, according to the readings, was real. Total and real, and it is through that resurrected body that the energy can be focused, can be directed, can become available, and is available to each and every one of us. I have used, and I will use again, an illustration: When you were a child, you took a magnifying glass and went out and focused the sun through that magnifying glass on a leaf, on a piece of paper, on a piece of cloth. You watched it begin to smolder. Smoke came up, and suddenly a flame burst from the sun's light focused. The resurrected body of Jesus is like that magnifying glass. When you and I focus it in our lives, it will set us on fire.

# The Resurrected Christ

In 1940, Edgar Cayce had a dream around 3:00 in the morning. Here is how he related it:

"Someone came to me and said: 'Do you want to go to a meeting?' I said, 'I don't know, I don't go out very much.' The person said to me, 'This is a very unusual meeting, I think you will enjoy it.' I asked, 'Who is going to be there?' He said, 'The Master is going to speak.' We went to the meeting, and it was the most beautiful place I have ever seen in my life. We entered a dark hallway, but not a long hall. The light in it was very dark blue, opalescent, and made our flesh look purple. As I looked at the people, I realized that all of them had passed on—no one was there in the flesh except myself. I didn't know the person who had asked me to come. With me and around me were mostly preachers—Mr. Moody, Mr. Smith, Mr. Jones, and many of those who had been ministers in the earth, and ones I had known. I couldn't see the light, but realized that it came from a Voice that spoke. No one was sitting. There were no benches or chairs. Everyone was standing. All were dressed in robes. It was the Lord speaking—but He could not be seen. He said, 'Who will go to bring peace again on earth?' Then Jesus stepped forward, and said: 'I will go. It is time for Me to go again into the earth to strengthen My brethren; [though] not to be born in the earth. . .'" (294-189 Supplement)

Men have been expecting the return of Jesus the Christ from the time that He died. The disciples expected it almost immediately. History tells us that just 1,000 years after Jesus, all of southern Europe didn't plant any crops because they thought the world was coming to an end and Jesus was going to return.

I have read in the newspapers from time to time of groups who have a revelation and expect Jesus to return. They sell everything they own. Such a group in Ohio back in the '20s did this. They were quite a large community of persons who sold everything, dressed in white robes, went up on a hill near them, and waited on a special morning that their leader had told them would be the end of the world, when Jesus would return. There are groups all over our nation, in fact, in many parts of the world, who are preaching that He is coming, who are expecting the Second Coming. Any new catastrophe or concern or worry brings further excitement about this time.

Let's go back, though, for a moment because this is a perplexing concern for us all. I suspect that if I questioned others individually and carefully, I would not find two people who would agree on what they think is going to happen. I certainly doubt I could find two people who would agree on a time. I'm not even sure that I could find two who would agree on how or on what kind of body was going to be used. What's the position of the Cayce readings on this? Let's examine a few selections:

*Q-3. What is meant by "the day of the Lord is near at hand"?*
A-3. That as has been promised through the prophets and the sages of old, the time—and half time—has been and is being fulfilled in this day and generation, and that soon there will again appear in the earth that one through whom many will be called to meet those that are preparing the way for His day in the earth. The Lord, then, will come, "even as ye have seen Him go."
*Q-4. How soon?*
A-4. When those that are His have made the way clear, *passable,* for Him to come.                                    262-49

. . .if ye will believe that He is, ye may experience. For as many as have named the name, and that do unto their brethren the deeds that bring to them. . .that closeness, oneness of purpose with Him, may know—ye, too—in body, in mind, that He *lives* TODAY, and will come and receive you unto Himself, that where He is there ye may be also. . .

For thy Christ, thy Lord, thy Jesus, is nigh unto thee—just now!                                                           5749-6

Then again He may come in body to claim His own. Is He abroad today in the earth? Yea, in those that cry unto Him from every corner; for He, the Father, hath not suffered His soul to see corruption; neither hath it taken hold on those things that make the soul afraid. For, He *is* the Son of Light, of God, and is holy before Him. And He comes again in the hearts and souls and minds of those that seek to know His ways.

These be hard to be understood by those in the flesh, where prejudice, avarice, vice of all natures holds sway in the flesh; yet those that call on Him will not go empty-handed. . .5749-5

What kind of body could He use? What about this return that is of interest to us? You and I have read about—and some of you may have personally experienced—an out-of-body experience, or meditation or dream experience that is *so* real you know it is not just of the mind but a part of yourself that can leave the flesh body and travel.

You read about these in parapsychology journals. They have also been written about by Dr. Raymond Moody in a book called *Life After Life,* in which he describes the experiences of people who died and were brought back to consciousness. They seemed, in that temporary state of death, to have a body that can perceive, look at, and move away from the flesh. Dr. Moody has recorded the experiences of hundreds of people—children as well as adults—moving in action and coming into the presence of a lighted figure which they thought was the Christ.

Let me show you what I mean. Quite a few people have had out-of-body experiences or dreams in which they felt a part of themselves moved out—sometimes they could see or perceive at a distance away—from their bodies.

Is this the body that Jesus is going to use or will He use something else? Did He use that finer body and just slow it down after the resurrection, when He began to appear to people around there? Do you question the accounts of those people? It's written carefully in Scripture that many people saw Him. He was seen on the road to Emmaus and in the garden. Many did not recognize Him until He had talked a while or, as with those on the road to Emmaus, until they sat down to eat. Then again He appeared to the disciples in the Upper Room. Thomas, who wasn't present, didn't believe it, so Jesus reappeared and let him examine His nail prints and the spear wound in His side. He told them He was going to Galilee, and they went out fishing. They had decided that nothing was going to happen, that He had gone, finally—so they thought. Then He appeared again. They saw Him on the shore at Galilee. He built a fire and began cooking fish. They saw Him and suddenly began to recognize the Master.

It's my personal opinion that Jesus so spiritualized the flesh that He moved the whole flesh body into another dimension. What He was using at this point was the spiritualized real body. Now, we've pointed out many times that this body, the flesh body, is changing all the time. But there is a patterned body and it was this body that He used to speed up so that He was able to take the flesh along with it. Whenever you come in contact with a body in another dimension, it's moving so fast that it has to slow down so you can see it. It is very much like an airplane propeller, which you can't see when it is turning at a certain speed; but as it slows down, you can begin to see a blur and finally you see the propeller clearly. So, what they saw in the beginning was a blur; that is, they knew it was a body but didn't know to whom it belonged.

But He was beginning to quicken their memories. Remember, you and I are not even the same bodies that we were a few minutes ago. If we didn't remember what we all looked like, we would be so completely changed by the end of the week that we wouldn't recognize each other. It is only our memories that we retain.

Change is where it's at; it's the order of the day. Everything is changing faster than we can possibly imagine. Now, it seems to me that the resurrected body of Jesus had control of this change, this energy pattern, and He could speed it up or slow it down. This process is a matter of spiritualizing the mental structure of every cell in the body, and it takes time. It is a gradual purification, until the mind of the cell is impregnated, filled with, a consciousness of its relationship to the creative power of the universe, or God.

This is done gradually, step by step, bit by bit, cell by cell. There are billions and billions of cells in our bodies, and we come again and again to get that done. Now, it would seem that Jesus did that, too. He came many times—and this may disturb some of you—many times into the earth.

If the body, that flesh body that He occupied as Jesus, had reached that point through many earthly incarnations in which He actually became a pattern for mankind, then He would set up an understanding of the laws that—if followed—would help us begin to move in consciousness, as He said, back to the point where He was. Was he saying this to us in the story of the Prodigal Son, that we are all in this sense prodigal sons and can return to our Father's house? Are we in that process? Do we have, with this figure, not just the Jesus of Christianity but a figure with an immense time span—from Adam right on up—in which He had, with every appearance, focused the world on the worship of the one God? A figure who worked with mankind, gradually guiding, helping and setting a pattern that we could follow?

There are signs—good signs—in this time of ours, even with all the shortages and confusions and threats of war—all the silliness with which we have involved ourselves. With our beginning to destroy our environment, it looks as if we will truly need a place to go. The way we're using and misusing the earth, we're making it almost untenable.

In these times are there also good signs? There is the tremendous growth of interest in the spiritual life. Hundreds of thousands of people all over the world are meditating and praying. New revivals and a new upsurging of religion give humanity an opportunity for a personal experience, a personal confrontation with God.

I have seen tremendous movements of people. I was amazed at what was going on in Brazil, in Sao Paulo, in the spiritist movement there. A strange mixture and confusion with Catholic influences—a belief in reincarnation, communication with the dead—all at the same time, and any one of them is enough to blow a person's mind. But *masses* of them are searching. One hundred thousand people sat in a big stadium with many so-called mediums who were talking with people on the other side. Also the growth of the fundamentalist movement in this country is absolutely amazing!

People are being reached over television with prayer and healing. The tremendous healing missions that have spread abroad exemplify people's beliefs, their need and desire to believe. The growth of young people's interest in the spiritual life has been remarkable, and they're continuing to search. Growth of interest in the whole field of parapsychology has been spectacular; the new spiritual energies and concepts of mankind show our ability to reach beyond normal perception. And it's not just in our country, but all over the world.

Recently, I listened to a kahuna in Hawaii. You would have thought he was giving a reading from the Edgar Cayce records about the changes that are upon us—not just upheavals, but the tremendous spiritual changes.

Let's look at this in another way:

. . .all power in heaven, in earth, is given to Him who overcame. Hence He is of Himself in space, in the force that impels through faith, through belief, in the individual entity. As a spirit entity. Hence not in a body in the earth, but may come at will to him who *wills* to be one with, and acts in love to make same possible.                                              5749-4

Jesus in space? A spiritual entity not incarnated in the earth, but able to come at will to whomever so desires? Does that sound familiar? Does that sound a little like "I stand at the door, and knock"? (Revelation 3:20) But it's only when we begin to expand our consciousness to break through our concepts and the bindings of time/space that we begin to sense and understand what takes place, and open the door. It is a door-opening process.

The doors of the mind, of the unconscious, are multitudinous. I have spent years talking with young people about drug experiences. Those people got some doors open; it blew their minds. It may even have changed the tissue of their bodies that will take years to replace properly, to reconnect all the nerve ends and synapses involved. But they had visions which started them on some strange searchings. Some of them went insane and are still confined; but many have found a spiritual path. The doors, they know, can be opened, but there are safer, better ways, which is what we are talking about here.

For, He shall come as ye have seen Him go, in the *body* He occupied in Galilee. The body that He formed, that was crucified on the cross, that rose from the tomb, that walked by the sea, that appeared to Simon, that appeared to Philip. . .
5749-4

In another reading Edgar Cayce uses a beautiful symbol: water.

As has been indicated, things material are the shadows of that which is spiritual in its essence.

Now He gave, "I am the breath of life—I am the water of life—he that drinks shall never thirst."

What meaneth this? How may it be put into words that one may grasp the meaning of what it means for that Spirit of the Christ—as manifested in Jesus—to be present as it were in a million places, as ye say, at once?

Now ye experience that $H_2O$ is water—everywhere! Then water is water, and a part of the whole, with all the essential elements that make for the ability of manifestations in bringing life, in quenching the thirst. And it becomes active thus in *whatever* sphere or phase it finds itself; whether in the frigid, as ice; in the temperate, as water; or in that phase as steam. Yet *everywhere*—in *every phase*—its activities are the same! And it may be illustrated as shown; three-fourths of the earth, three-fourths of man, three-fourths of all matter we find a composition of that which He gave *is* a manifestation of His presence, His force, His influence!

Then it may be understood as the individual entity grasps that idea that it is as we deal, as we mete, as we measure to our fellow man, that the water of life flows through us.

Hence how applicable becomes that as He gave, "He that gives a cup of water in my name shall in no manner lose his reward!"                                                    1158-12

Three-fourths of the earth is water; three-fourths of you and me, at the flesh level, is water. Water is used here also probably as a symbol of that strange period in time. (Edgar Cayce was a Piscean, you know, and his "fish" had to have something in which to swim.) As we deal with, as we mete, as we measure to our fellow man, the water of life flows through us. It is a symbol of that which gives life to the earth, life to our bodies. We are born in water, we are composed of water. It symbolizes also the spiritual energy. "He that gives a cup of water [this energy of life, this water of life, this spiritual energy] in my name shall in no manner lose his reward!" (1158-12) We can give symbolically—as a cup, a prayer, a smile, a word of encouragement, a touch of a hand, a healing thought, a constructive hopeful thought.

For when ye walk with Him, in purpose and in ideal, ye will find that ye are never alone. Think not that ye or any other individual may be the only one serving a living God. For since His entry into the world, and His making it possible for man to find his way back to God, there has been and will continue to be an increase. For God has not willed that any soul should perish. Though the lights of hope may oft grow dim, in the violence that is created by those who become self-conscious of ability and who use self and others for gratifying of selfish desires, let it ever be said of thee that ye will make, ye will cause the welkin to ring for the glory of the coming of the Lord. For He will one day come again, and thou shalt see Him as He is, even as thou hast seen in thy early sojourns the glory of the day of the triumphal entry and the day of the crucifixion, and as ye also heard the angels proclaim "As ye have seen Him go, so will ye see Him come again."                              3615-1

To quote from another reading: "Search deep into the heart, the soul of self, and see from whence cometh that motivating force that *drives* self on to activity." (487-17) Look at the self. What is the purpose, the motive? What moves you? Is it to pattern the life to serve God or is it something on your own, your own little trip? That which *"drives* self on to activity"? Understand this. Look at it. Try to understand it.

If it is for laudation of self alone, if it is for the

aggrandizement of the interests in material things alone, then know—while you may materially succeed—the *ends* thereof are not well. But seek through those activities that bring the analyzing of same in the human body, in the human relationships, that may be spiritualized by the desires of the heart—and ye will find joy and peace, and—yea—in those days—when His forerunner may come into the earth for preparing the place for the Son of man, that His kingdom may be established in the earth, wilt thou be ready? Seek ye Him.

487-17

Then, as that coming into the world in the second coming— for He will come again and receive His own, who have prepared themselves through that belief in Him and acting in the manner; for the *Spirit* is abroad, and the time draws near, and there will be the reckoning of those even as in the first so in the last, and the last shall be first; for there is that Spirit abroad—He standeth near. He that hath eyes to see, let him see. He that hath ears to hear, let him hear that music of the coming of the Lord of this vineyard, and art *thou* ready to give account of that *thou* hast done with thine opportunity in the earth as the Sons of God, as the heirs and joint heirs of glory *with* the Son? Then make thine paths straight, for there must come an answering for that *thou* has done with thine Lord!

364-7

You know, if you couldn't think of any other reason for having prayer and meditation in your life now as a daily discipline, this would be good enough. I wouldn't take any chances on that. Cayce might be just seeing something here that is imminent. The Son prepared the way so that all people might know the love of the Father. ". . .then do with a might that thy hands find to do to make for the greater manifestations of the love of the Father in the earth." (262-58) Do it! Think it! If you can't think of something that deals with manifesting the love of the Father that is flowing and can flow through you, then keep your mouth shut!

And as ye would be the channel to hasten that glorious day of the coming of the Lord, then do with a might that thy hands find to do to make for the greater manifestations of the love of the Father in the earth. For, into thy keeping, and to His children and to His sons, has He committed the keeping of the saving of the world, of the souls of men. . .                    262-58

This is why I keep repeating that we have no other reason for being.

Then, as there is prepared the way by those that have made and do make the channels for the entering in, there may come into the earth those influences that will save, regenerate, resuscitate, *hold*—if you please—the earth in its continued activity toward the proper understanding and proper relationships to that which is the making for the closer relationships to that which is in Him *alone*.          5749-5

What Edgar Cayce is saying is that it is possible that our action, our thought, our prayer, our work will save, regenerate, resuscitate, hold the earth in place in its continued activity toward the proper understanding and proper relationships for the closer walk with Him.

Ye have seen it in Adam; ye have heard it in Enoch, ye have had it made known in Melchizedek; Joshua, Joseph, David, and those that made the preparation then for Him called Jesus. Ye have seen His Spirit in the leaders in all realms of activity, whether in the isles of the sea, the wilderness, the mountain, or in the various activities of every race, every color, every activity of that which has produced and does produce contention in the minds and hearts of those that dwell in the flesh.
For, what must be obliterated? Hate, prejudice, selfishness, backbiting, unkindness, anger, passion, and those things of the mire that are created in the activities of the sons of men.
5749-5

We must obliterate hate—not in other people—in ourselves. Prejudice—not in others—in ourselves. Selfishness—not changing others, but changing ourselves. The same goes for backbiting, unkindness, anger, passion—"those things of the mire that are created in the activities of the sons of men." (5749-5) Maybe I didn't cover your particular problem, but I bet I hit a few of you. I didn't have any trouble finding myself there either!

Then again He may come in body to claim His own. Is He abroad today in the earth? Yea, in those that cry unto Him from every corner; for He, the Father, hath not suffered His soul to see corruption; neither hath it taken hold on those things that make the soul afraid. For, He *is* the Son of Light, of God, and is holy before Him. And He comes again in the hearts and souls and minds of those that seek to know His ways.
5749-5

To continue: "These be hard to be understood by those in the flesh, where prejudice, avarice, vice of all natures hold sway in the flesh; yet those that call on Him will not go empty-handed—even as thou, in thine ignorance, in thine zealousness that has at times eaten thee up." (5749-5) Edgar Cayce is speaking to an individual here, but he might as well be speaking to many of us, who may at times be eaten up by our own zealousness. "Yet *here* ye may hear the golden sceptre ring—ring—in the hearts of those that seek His face. Ye, too, may minister in those days when He will come in the flesh, in the earth, to call His own by name." (5749-5)

This is quite a challenge. Let me see if I can put a personal experience of mine in a frame of reference so that you can sense the way I believe in it and think about it. Some years ago I was on a lecture trip, driving and staying in homes en route. I became ill and had to go to bed in the home where I was staying. A doctor had to make a house call. Now, a group of people were invited to that home that night, and I was supposed to give a talk. I insisted upon getting up. I was delirious and feverish. At that time the A.R.E. had only a few hundred members and most of the readings had not been indexed. Very few doctors were keeping any sort of records and no books had been written.

I got up and spoke, but I don't know what I said. It didn't make much difference because, as I spoke, Someone came and stood near me, reached out and touched me. I stopped talking and stared and came apart. He laughed at me and in effect—not in words—said, "Get to work!" Everything that has happened has moved from that moment in the most amazing fashion in ways I could not have possibly dreamt of. Doors have opened in ways I could not possibly have conceived of in my wildest imagination. I fell down many times, but it's much easier to get up just by remembering that moment and that smile. "It is I." I didn't tell anybody about that experience, so a lot of people wondered what went on.

We all have a work to do. Let me close with two quotes from the Edgar Cayce work readings:

. . .for the time has arisen in the earth when men—everywhere—seek to know more of the *mysteries* of the mind, the soul, the *soul's* mind—which man recognizes as existent, yet has seen little of the *abilities* of same.          254-52

Well that those that now labor in same carry on, that there may be the foundation laid of the work to be accomplished in and through the Association; for into thy hands has been committed the keeping of those records—yes, those conditions that are as records—of the foundation of that upon which the better understanding of man's relation to the all-creative energy within self may be made manifest in the earth's plane at this period. Keep that committed unto thy keeping against that day when there will be said, "Well done," according to that as enacted in this present experience. With the coming of the dawn many will call thee blessed.                254-43

This reading is not to an individual, but to every soul who aligns himself or herself with this purpose, this pattern, of this man we call Jesus. Let's get to work in following this pattern that He's laid before us. We think it's pretty straight and hard, but holding on to Him and walking in the light, it will be easier. And all the little worlds in which we live will, I think, be better places.

# Jesus the Christ

We are going to explore together several of the concepts that Jesus dealt with. I want to examine some extracts from the Edgar Cayce readings and pause and discuss these with you. The perspective of the readings is not something that you have to accept or swallow completely, but rather something to stretch your mind a bit through some of the concepts that are presented here. Nowhere in the Cayce readings was my mind so stretched, personally, as in this area which involves the universality of the Christ concept.

In one reading Edgar Cayce said, "So attune thyselves that ye may harken, not as to an experience only. . ." (281-25) Now, you and I have been hung up for years looking for "an experience." So frequently we see people trying to meditate who are looking for an experience, who want a light or a vision, or want some guidance or direction of some kind of where to go. We want to have an experience instead of accepting this approach of the readings, "but rather *live* and *be* the experience in the hearts of those that are seeking to find their way. . ." (281-25)

You see, it's the changes that are made in your life that enable you to live and be the experience. It's your new attitude, your new way of speaking, your new way of thinking, your getting rid of the criticism and the condemnation and the self-pity, and the things that block you from *serving*.

We are all so filled with the God energy that we are each capable of far, far more than any of us ever dreamed we were. We begin to see what Jesus meant when He said, "Greater things than I have done, you can do." (See John 14:12.) Then we, in meditation, are to seek to apply and change and become—not to see something, not to hear something or to have a particular kind of experience. Remember, meditation is a cleansing. It is an attunement of the body and the mind with the spiritual purpose, and the awakening of spiritual goals, so that we begin to direct our lives with spiritual goals and spiritual principles rather than the ego trip we are all taking every day of our lives. We all have our own particular poison, which we take regularly in our thoughts, words and actions.

Let's examine how we may move away from this.

Edgar Cayce says that it is in service, of course, that you change, so that you can then help "in the hearts of those that are seeking to find their way; whether in the troubles of the body, of the mind, or whether they are lost among those turmoils of the cry, 'This way—that way'...Be the experience to someone to light their lives, their bodies, their minds to thy *living* Lord, thy Brother, the Christ! For He has promised in His words in thine own heart, that keeps the hope, that keeps the fires of thine own heart aflame, 'Ye finding me may know the *joy* of the Lord.'" (281-25)

Now, how do we do this? There is not a one of us who would not try to look toward what we vaguely call the Christ Consciousness. It is in the misalignment of our bodies that our minds become befuddled and distorted. The voices we hear are the voices of the lower self—what we call the "devil" in us— then they become mixed and mingled until we cannot hear the principles.

As we begin to seek, through meditation and prayer, to align and attune, we need to balance the body and to control the mind. We begin to be able to turn loose and be cleansed of the karmic patterns that we carry in the emotional body, to turn loose of these thought patterns to which we cling and onto which we hold.

What is the Christ Consciousness and how do we attain to it? Of course, it's the fruits of the spirit. We've got to be more gentle, a little kinder, a little more patient, a little more thoughtful, and bring a little more peace into the lives of those we touch every day, if we are to emulate this example of Jesus who became the Christ—and we don't have any other reason for existence, as I see it, in all this universe. This is what it's all about. This is why you're here. This is why you keep knocking against one another in trying to find some way. It's too simple.

In this next reading Cayce spoke to a particular group, but I think he also spoke to all of us:

As many of you served there, as many experienced those purifications for an active service among their fellow man in an *individual* experience, so may ye purify thy minds and thy bodies. . .that thy *mind* may put ON Christ, the garments of a living Lord, that ye may be not as ones stumbling, as ones fearful of this or that, but *sure* and *certain* in the joys of a risen Lord; that indeed thy body in its expressions may be the Temple *Beautiful* for thy *living* Lord.　　　　**281-25**

You know, the problem that we face is that we're willing to give a little bit of the self, but it's hard for us to give all of it, the body and the mind, to turn loose and *be* rather than strive to "experience" something. It's walking the way, not just knowing about the way. This effort requires a moment-by-moment, day-by-day application of what we know of spiritual law. Fortunately, I am not required to obey what someone else knows or has been living, but I am required to obey what I accept as spiritual law. And so are you required to obey what you individually accept as spiritual law. That's all. Then you begin to move and change and grow toward God consciousness.

Edgar Cayce goes on, "He thy brother, thy Christ, hath given that God is God of the *living* way." (281-25) Is this living way some vague highway, some mystical path? I don't think so. I think it's the peace and the calmness, the kind word, the cup of water, the thoughtfulness, the patience, and all the little things that go to make up the everyday experience of being more Christ-like.

There was a constant flow of spiritual energy through Jesus. A number of times I have stated my opinion that Jesus in His resurrected form, His resurrected body, has provided a kind of magnifying glass through which the God energy shines, and, like that magnifying glass, if you focus it in your life, it'll set you on fire and change you. It'll burn up and consume that which you have builded that is in the way. It will bring up your creative capacities and abilities so that you begin to serve and help in ways you never dreamed of in the earth.

Healing is a multifaceted operation. You have known times when a smile healed and made all the difference in the world in your life. Each of us has known times when the pat of a hand from a friend or the touch of a hand from a mother or father changed our lives, or when somebody grabbed us and hugged us at the right time or kissed away a tear. We are all still children in this sense.

Healing is not just related to the confusions of our body cells, our flesh cells, but is concerned with our emotions and thought forms. It concerns the whole finer body which is so susceptible to prayer. Our understanding of time is a factor here, too. You and I think we want something right now, but there isn't any *now*—just the total picture. So a prayer works, a smile or a word of encouragement works, maybe not as your conscious mind sees that it should, but it goes on in time. The famous illustration of the seed is so important here. After you've planted it, you mustn't keep digging it up or it won't really grow very well. Just so, our healing is a constant daily thought process—a constructive, not a negative, thought. We are so accustomed to framing the negative rather than the positive, constructive thought—in thought, then in word, and then in action. Healing is an ongoing thing.

Now when we draw together in small or large groups, we amplify the spiritual energy. We are all custodians of this energy. It's one energy, God's, flowing through us. It's nothing we do, but it flows through us. As we come together, it builds up and builds up, and there's tremendous capacity for healing. In an A.R.E. Search for God Study Group, at the end of the meeting, when the group has healing prayer following the meditation, automatically the energy flows to where there is the greatest need and it is magnified and multiplied by the group. This is "where two or three are gathered. . .in my name . . ." (Matthew 18:20)

Do you say God is remiss, that He hasn't gotten around to giving, channeling the spiritual energy through you to heal? Or is it that there is something in you that's still blocking it and not really opening up? I think we are making reference here to the way to bring this focus about. Jesus' resurrected body becomes for mankind that magnifying glass through which we can begin to see the creative power of the universe more clearly in action than ever before. The living way is being more Christ-like.

Jesus is a pattern for us, a way. "And as there is the analyzing of the Christ Life, Christ Consciousness, one realizes and finds that the Christ Child was born into the earth as man; one born in due season, in due time, in man's spiritual evolution, that man might have a pattern of the personality and the individuality of God Himself." (5758-1) It's a pattern, a way, an attitude to take, the kind of thoughts to think, the action, the decisions, the direction of one's life. We need patterns to follow.

. . .it is ever those that draw nearer to the universal consciousness of the Christ that come closer to the perfect relationship to the Creative Forces or God, the Father—which the man Jesus attained when He gave of Himself to the world, that through Him, by and in Him, each entity might come to know the true relationship with the Father.          3357-2

And another reading: "THE WAY is that manifested in the creative forces through Jesus, the Christ, the Son, for He *is* the way, the truth, the light, in which the body, the mind, the soul may find that security, that understanding, that comprehending of the oneness of the spiritual *within* material, that is manifested in every individual." Now this is a tremendous challenge. It would hurt no one to try this to see whether or not it would work. What is this reading saying? It is saying that in this concept of Jesus who became the Christ is something in which the body, the mind, and the soul may find security and understanding and comprehension of the oneness.

We sense scientifically the oneness of everything but, when we try to experience it, things get separated. We're creatures of experience, constantly recording an amazing input of stimuli via the five senses, and we separate and compartmentalize everything. Then oneness goes out the window in our experience. So, we have to turn within and find ways in which this oneness can be understood and experienced in our lives. The readings suggest that it can be done through finding, looking at, and then obeying and working with the laws that Jesus the Christ manifested.

[Jesus] becomes, then as the elder brother, to all who are *born* in the earth, as the maker, as the creator, as the first, as the last; as the beginning, and as the end of man's soul's experience through the earth and throughout the spheres of consciousness in and about the earth. Thus is He the only begotten, the first born, the first to know flesh, the first to purify it.

1158-5

According to these readings, you and I are citizens of the universe, not just citizens of the earth. What we call the earth plane and the experience here is just a trip—about the heaviest trip we've taken in quite a while!—but just a trip. Out of this trip that we've gotten into, God is choosing to make His ways possible and known even in the experience of humanity. There was actually a projection and movement of the God consciousness into matter back in the beginning when there needed to be a pattern set up. This soul that we came to know as Jesus entered again and again to show a pattern, a way, by which we can come back to a consciousness of what we had with Him before the world was.

Jesus who became the Christ was the first of the projections of God consciousness into matter, the first-born in the earth, the first to know flesh and then, knowing flesh, the first to purify it, to resurrect it.

"Thus it became necessary that God in His goodness give an

example, a pattern, by which man might conduct his life, his ideals, his hopes, his fears, all of his idiosyncracies—a pattern laid out for man. Those who accept same may live in peace and harmony with themselves and others." What an opportunity! Accept this pattern and live in peace and harmony. It's worth trying! "Those who reject same continue to find discordant notes with their own associates and with every activity of life there is continued trouble." That's a strange statement here and quite a promise. Many times we say, "Why me, Lord, why me? Everything happens to me!" When we find these discordant notes in our lives, we might ask ourselves, "What is thy pattern?"

Here is yet another statement about Jesus from the readings: "Throughout the experience of man in the material world, at various seasons and periods, teachers or 'would-be' teachers have come; setting up certain forms or certain theories as to manners in which an individual shall control the appetites of the body or of the mind, so as to attain to some particular phase of development. There has also come a teacher who was bold enough to declare Himself as the Son of the living god." (And who says that you and I are that also. That's the challenge!) "He set no rules of appetite. He set no rules of ethics, other than 'as ye would that men should do to you, do ye even so to them,' and to know 'Inasmuch as ye do it unto the least of these, thy brethren, ye do it unto thy Maker.'" (357-13)

We worship God, but we choke the daylights out of our neighbors. So we deal with God one way with one hand and deal with God another way with the other hand and think we can get away with it.

Jesus declared that the kingdom of heaven is within each individual. It takes consciousness to be aware of, through meditation, the fact that God is the Father of every soul. "He came to demonstrate, to manifest, to give light and life to all. Here, then, ye find a friend, a brother, a companion. As He gave, 'I call ye not servants, but brethen.' For, as many as believe, to them He gives power to become the children of God. . ." (357-13)

This discourse may sound like a sermon to you at this point. You've heard it before, but you probably haven't heard it with the emphasis on our wholeness: the body, the mind, and the soul as one with the Father, "joint heirs with this Jesus, the Christ, in the knowledge and in the awareness of this presence abiding ever with those who set this ideal before them." (357-13)

Then again from the readings: "For the Master, Jesus, even

the Christ, is the pattern for every man in the earth, whether he be Gentile or Jew, Parthenian or Greek. For all have the pattern, whether they call on that name or not; but there is no other name given under heaven whereby men may be saved from themselves." (3528-1) That last phrase is a happy one, I think. You and I have great fears and are disturbed about what other people can do to us. If we extend that and get a little metaphysically inclined, we begin to hatch up some devils, some evil spirits, and all kinds of things to grab us. In reality, though, the saving is from ourselves. We create the attractions, the patterns, the blocks, and the destruction. And all these must be cleansed.

To me this is why the cleansing aspect of meditation is so important. The blocks begin gradually to fall away, so slowly sometimes we don't recognize that they're going. A fit of anger or irritation begins to go, and you find greater peace. You find you're not opening your mouth so often and pitying yourself and explaining what horrible shape you're in and how difficult it is. Slowly these blocks slide away as we press on toward this mark of the higher calling. Our consciousness begins to move and expand in terms of a more universal outlook on life.

"In analyzing self, the entity finds itself body, mind and soul that answers in three-dimensional plane to the Godhead, the Father, the Son and the Holy Spirit.

"Then, be one—in thy purpose. Know, as given of old, the man called Jesus is the Savior of the world. He has purchased with His own will that right for direction. And He has promised, 'I will never leave thee—I will not forsake thee,' save that *thou*—as an individual—cast Him out, or reject Him for counsel from some other source." (2970-1)

How is it possible that He will never leave us? In our times it is not difficult at all for the World Series to come into every living room in millions of homes all over the world. How can we doubt that the resurrected body of Jesus cannot do this? If we turn the switch on, if we tune in to it, how can we doubt it? Unfortunately, the little television set within us that we are turning up and tuning in is not a one-knob operation. There's static and a lot of knobs in us so that a lot of attunements are necessary. Then we begin to tune in to this pattern of Jesus. Slowly, yes, through meditation, but also through the discipline of our wills, we choose the spiritual laws that we know to live. We tune in until He begins to come and touch our lives.

66

In Jesus, who became the Christ, you have a pattern, you have an example. Study them to show yourself approved unto that standard. Know that His promises to man as to His relationships to things in the earth, to things about the individual, to his Maker, to the heavenly Father, are true. For as He gave, "Though the heavens and the earth may pass away, my words shall *not* pass away—but shall be *fulfilled* EVERY WHIT. 1089-7

And it's literally that: every whit.

# The Cross and the Crown

The small group of people who worked with Edgar Cayce took three months of study to put together the material in "The Cross and the Crown" chapter of *A Search for God,* Book I. Since then, many groups who come to their study of this chapter have dissolved because they couldn't deal with it. I'm not sure of all the reasons, but I think some of them will become apparent as we begin to examine a few of the concepts here.

You know, you can be ambling along through life wondering what it's all about and you can be working with ideas and concepts out of the readings, then suddenly you come face to face with the need to take a stand. Here's the crossroad, the point where you've got to make a decision. You must take a definite stand and the stand has to be: "For I determined not to know any thing among you, save Jesus Christ, and him crucified." (I Corinthians 2:2)

At that point your whole concept of Jesus needs to come into focus again—to be rethought, re-examined—and a decision has to be made. *A Search for God* and the Edgar Cayce readings suggest a universal concept of the Christ Consciousness. Since it is not a narrow, orthodox kind of concept, it gives one a lot of room, a lot of leeway. But this is the point where you take a stand, where you make up your mind. Some people, however, may not be ready.

One may ask at this point, "Why choose the way of the cross?" What is a cross? A symbol of shame, a symbol of pain and suffering. Why the cross? Why is it necessary to deal with suffering? Why must you and I come to grips with this concept of suffering? Can we, in some way, magically erase all suffering? Is that what it's about? Are we going to get rid of it all? If God is only goodness and love, then why is it necessary to have suffering? Why must you yourself or your child suffer in the earth?

The way Jesus chose is the way of service, the way of sacrifice, the way of selflessness. As we examine this concept of suffering, we observe these three aspects: physical, mental, and spiritual.

Where did suffering come from, why is it here, and why do we have to deal with it? All philosophies and all religions have tried to approach this in several different manners. We are going to speak about it as *His* way—that is, the way of God, the way of Jesus the Christ in the earth or God in the earth. It is the way of service, the way of sacrifice, the way of selflessness. Now if one is on an "ego trip," you can see what a tremendous blow to the ego it would be to run head on into this.

"We come to realize that, in fact, there is no other name given among men whereby we can be saved from self except through Him." (ASFG, I, p. 104) Now what does that mean? Isn't Jesus just a great teacher? Isn't He one of many spiritual leaders in the world and can't we just accept Him that way? Why must He be the way through which we can be saved from ourselves? We have to come up with some answers on that.

He showed that His way is the way of love, a matter of taking up one's cross daily. We emulate Jesus' example by doing likewise and desiring more and more to help others. What is the cross then? A way of love—yet a way of taking up and dealing with suffering. The cross as an image of suffering symbolizes the self, the ego. It becomes, then, a symbol of that which must be borne and overcome in every life.

"Though he were a Son, yet learned he obedience by the things which he suffered. . ." (Hebrews 5:8) We have all heard that often, yet we have also heard it said, "I don't need to deal with suffering. I'm going to erase all of that." Or "Everything is perfect, everything is beautiful, everything is good. I don't have to deal with suffering." Has He done it all for us? Wiped it all out? Certainly the church has been telling us this for a long time: Believe and be saved.

Why is it necessary, then, to bear a cross? Just because it was borne by Him? The reason is that you and I, the spiritual beings that we are, found gratification in the lower forms of vibration. So we meet again and again the seeds we have sown, and we come to realize that it is only through overcoming them that we can ever hope to regain that from which we have fallen. Rebirth is the opportunity given to the sons of men by which this may be accomplished. A return to the state of consciousness of oneness with God—a moving out of this lower vibration, a re-establishment of our original relationship with God—may be accomplished through rebirth. It is the way of return.

The law of cause and effect is evidenced today in the material, the mental, and the spiritual world; but in overcoming the world, the law, He became the law. The law, then, becomes a schoolmaster or a school of training—not a punishment. The earth becomes a school. This reminds me of a story: A little boy who had been in school a whole year was speaking to his younger brother, who was just starting school. He said, "Bobby, when you get to school and they try to teach you how to spell that word 'cat,' don't you learn it. Because if you learn that first one, they get harder and harder from then on. So don't do the first one." Sometimes you and I also get the feeling that as we move and begin working with the first laws, it starts to get harder and harder.

Because this earth is a school, we need to understand what we're doing here: We're helping to bring the consciousness of man back to a consciousness of a relationship with God. Jesus showed the way back to God, and we imitate Him through our service to others. Often, however, when we begin to try to serve, we get hurt.

The Edgar Cayce readings suggest that the God Force became ensnared in matter. It is stated more fully in *A Search for God,* Book I: "The God Force became ensnared in matter and, in the first Adam, fell. It was necessary, therefore, that the God Force, the Creator, individualize Himself as an example and by overcoming the world become the Law, in order that man might know the way out. So, in the last Adam all are made alive." (ASFG, I, p. 106)

The suggestion here is that the figure we know as Jesus who became the Christ was the first and the last Adam. This is quite a thing to deal with. It's not something new, but very old. In other words, the one we came to know as Jesus had been here many times in the earth and had literally taken on this school, this way of suffering, this way of learning. Hence, "learned he obedience by the things which he suffered. . ." (Hebrews 5:8) Not just in one life, but in many, in the earth. And the first and the last was Adam.

Jesus actually alludes to His past lives several times. Once when He was speaking to a group of people about Abraham He said, "Abraham rejoiced to see my day: and he saw it, and was glad." (John 8:56) Some of the people thought, "What in the world is this man talking about? Abraham died centuries ago. How could he have known Abraham?" According to the Edgar Cayce readings, one of the incarnations of Jesus was Melchizedek. Perhaps this life is what Jesus was referring to.

You'll recall that Melchizedek was the prince of Salem, the one with whom Abraham broke bread and drank wine, and to whom he paid tithes. Salem, of course, means peace, so Melchizedek was also the prince of peace. So, we are suggesting that Jesus began in the earth plane as Adam and left as Jesus the Christ, having purified, perfected and moved to lay out a path, a lighted path, over which you and I could travel.

Now this path is a school and will bring into the earth a certain amount of wear and tear and what we call suffering, which He so clearly defined for us. The way is really easy if you choose it. He paved the way for everyone, so that through His strength all might come to the knowledge and understanding of the way, might be able to overcome all things and become kings and priests unto God. The earth is where we do it.

Now that's a big order. It's worth a little learning, a little working with the laws, a little suffering, if you will, that we through His strength understand the way and conquer all to become priests unto God. This is the challenge: to follow Him and achieve this.

What "blows our minds" is the idea that we might just be able to do it—some time, some place. To imagine that we are involved in this kind of exciting experience and movement in consciousness is mind-boggling. It astounds us that we are part of this bigger plan and not a bunch of unimportant ants crawling around on a little planet on the edge of a galaxy in the middle of the universe. Even more, what a dream, what a challenge, what an opportunity this sets forth! If we think about it, we begin to understand a little better what Jesus meant when He said, ". . .take up [your] cross, and follow me." (Matthew 16:24) Whatever you and I have to deal with which we have created and built in the earth, that we will face, and we will do so in His hour, in His light, and on that lighted way gladly, easily and joyously, when we choose. But we *must* choose to go this way—not be shoved or pushed into it.

I remember the story about a man who was praised for his great bravery. He had been a passenger on a large ship. At one point everybody was crowded at the rail looking at some dolphins in the water, when a very beautiful girl fell overboard. The oldest, most crotchety, most wizened-looking little man on the ship suddenly dived after her. He struggled in the water. Finally someone threw a life belt and he put the girl into it. Everyone cheered. That night at the big dinner celebration they all were extolling the bravery of this man. He was asked to stand up and give a speech. He said, "Ladies and gentlemen, I have but one question for you. Who pushed me?" You and I may feel a lot of times as if we're being pushed, but we must begin to learn to make choices.

Another challenging idea in the Cayce readings is that

through Jesus' thought and will humanity took physical form. Through Jesus who became the Christ—God-thought, in other words—and will, we took physical form so that we now would have an opportunity to deal with the situations we had created in the earth. He chose to take upon Himself the responsibilities of overcoming the physical, making Himself the law through fulfilling all the requirements. Remember John's statement, "In the beginning was the Word, and the Word was with God, and the Word was God. The same was in the beginning with God." (John 1:1-2) The Word came and dwelt among us, becoming the offspring of self in the material world. The Word overcame the world; hence, the world became like the servant of the One who overcame it. So Jesus came to that point at which He could help us see our course in a new light and we begin to catch a glimpse of the glory of the crown.

A crown is actually just a symbol of raised consciousness, though this meaning has really been lost somewhat. It was placed upon the head of one in a state of raised consciousness. This person was then given a rod, a scepter, and would touch people with it and they would be healed. In the Middle Ages thousands of people used to line up for the king to touch them on the head. Many of them were healed because they believed the king was in an exalted, ordained state of higher consciousness. The crown symbolized this raised consciousness and outgoing healing force. Even the stones in the crown were carefully selected to help pull the energies up to the head. Knowing this, we begin to make some sense of the meaning of the symbology.

The readings suggest that the cross is the emblem of Jesus' subjected self. It, then, became for Him the part of the self that had built the pattern in the earth that had to be overcome; so He overcame it for everybody. We usually consider the cross an emblem of shame, for innately we realize that it is symbolic of opposition to God's love. In other words, where we have built selfishness, gratified the self, built the ego, we sense that we have moved away from God's love and God's laws. We know we are not loving and are not serving as we should, so the cross innately becomes a symbol of shame.

As we meet the crosses, endure and overcome the temptations, we become heirs and joint heirs with Him to the crown of glory. All who fulfill the purpose for which they are called bear their crosses—not in sorrow, not in wailing, but in the joy of the Lord. It's hard for us to recognize, to believe, to accept, that suffering is of our making. Yet that's what hangs us up: there is *none* except of our making.

The readings explained this further: There is *nothing* between us and God, but the self which we have builded and created. It is self that is being met. This is what the cross is all about.

Now to handle all this is quite an operation! It forces you to rid yourself of your parents and the Russians, to rid yourself of society, God and the devil, and face up to this concept that *you* are responsible. You can see timid people shy away at this point. However, when you get to this point, don't run away. Grab this and try to work with it.

It is not in time or season or in any place, but in every place, every day and every hour, that we may show forth His love to those we contact. This idea is stated in the first affirmation of *A Search for God:* "Not my will but Thine, O Lord, be done in me and through me. Let me ever be a channel of blessings, today, now, to those that I contact in every way." (p. 22) It becomes that simple in this business of service.

By our lives others may know that He walks with us and is our Friend. Upon what is the glory of the crown based? Faithfulness to the desire to walk this lighted path that He set for us. So let us take up our cross and follow Him.

# Jesus Who Became the Christ

One day in 1934, after my mother had given Dad the suggestion to awaken from the reading he was giving, he said in a kind of awed tone, "Jesus of Nazareth passeth by. Let Him fill thine heart with the hopes of those promises that are indeed thine, wilt thou but apply. Trust ye in the Lord." (378-41) On waking up, Dad said that he had seen the Master walking down the road toward us—toward *all* of us. There was a group there and all of us were expectant and waiting for Him to come and He was smiling and seemed very happy.

Let's look at the concept of Jesus as we find it in the Edgar Cayce readings:

Then when there are those experiences in the life of an entity in the material plane, when expression is given to that which is the prompting or directing influence in the life of an individual entity, it is ever those that draw nearer to the universal consciousness of the Christ that come closer to the perfect relationship to the Creative Forces or God, the Father—which the man Jesus attained when He gave of Himself to the world, that through Him, by and in Him, each entity might come to know the true relationship with the Father...

At such times, then, look deep into the life of the man Jesus and see how He dealt with the problems of the day. As He gave, in the interpretation of His purpose in the earth, He recognized the needs of each soul as to its purpose in the earth also. For, all men (and He was a man) have fallen short of the glory of God. Only in Him, through Him, by Him may one attain to that true sonship, that true fellowship, that true relationship to the Creative Forces or God.           3357-2

Edgar Cayce moves in the readings from the idea of Jesus the man to Jesus who became the Christ, "Hold to the ideal, and that one that is set in Jesus who *became* the Christ." (1861-16)

In another he said, ". . .hold to that which *is* the criterion—'I am determined to know nothing among men save Jesus, the

Christ, and him crucified!' Not the man Jesus, but that which would keep men from knowing of that consciousness and promise that has been and is a part of every soul that seeks to know Him. For He indeed stands at the door of every consciousness of man that seeks to know; and will enter if man will but open." (1842-1)

Now, how do you and I look at Jesus? How have we been looking at Him? As a soul like us, created by God, who attained to Christ Consciousness? Is He just one of the bodies who got there first? Is it possible that He is the soul that led the descent into matter? Is He the "first begotten" of the Father, a special kind of creation, a special kind of energy pattern with a special job? Or is He an aspect of God—God Himself—in manifestation? Which of these do you hold, do you think about—and how do you work with those?

What do the readings say?

In that the man, Jesus, became...manifest in the world, and the will one with the Father, He became. . .from man's viewpoint...the only, the first, the begotten of the Father, and the ensample to the world, whether Jew, Gentile, or of any other religious forces.                      900-17

Hence as one reads or sees the interpretations of these in the life of Jesus of Nazareth, who became the Christ, the Savior, through fulfilling those purposes, one realizes that indeed He has become the way, the truth and the light.

Thus the individual entity finds that the body, or that first creation of God, the mind, is the way; or the way through which light may come to the entity of the Father. For, as are the pronouncements in the law by Moses, "Today there is set before thee good and evil, life and death. And say not who will descend from heaven to bring a message, or who may come from over the sea, for Lo, it is within thine own heart."

And how *well* this is completed in that promise, that pronouncement, that admonition given by Him as He led the way to fulfill in the garden and on the cross the law itself, to demonstrate that separation from God might indeed be broken away forever. As He gave, "In my Father's house are many mansions; if it were not so I would have told you. I go to prepare a place, that where I am, there ye may be also."

Thus we see the relationship each soul bears to the Father, as to the way, the Christ, by wholly trusting in Him day by day. As He said, "I stand continually at the door of thy heart. Open and I will enter."

How do ye open? Through searching, seeking, humbling thyself before the throne of grace and mercy, as was manifested in Him; acknowledging Him as thy Lord, thy Master, yea thy elder brother.

He has given also, "If ye open I will come and abide with thee."

This then, is the manner, the way, the truth, the light, through which this entity may find its true relationships to the Creative Forces. 2845-1

In such a manner may individuals become aware of the Christ Consciousness and become one with the operative forces of the Christ Spirit abroad in the earth; for He shall come again, even as ye have seen Him go. *Then* shall the Christ Spirit be manifest in the world, even as the Christ Consciousness may make thee aware of that promised as the Comforter in this material world.

Then, the Christ Consciousness is the Holy Spirit, or that as the promise of His presence made aware of His activity in the earth. The spirit is as the Christ in action with the Spirit of the Father. 262-29

And, as we've said, as the readings certainly suggest, this is a time when the Christ Spirit is abroad in the earth.

Edgar Cayce defined this Christ Consciousness again in another reading in this way: "The Christ Consciousness is a universal consciousness of the Father Spirit. The Jesus consciousness is that man builds as body worship." (5749-4)

He was asked this question, "Are heredity, environment and will equal factors in aiding or retarding the entity's development?"

"Will is the greater factor," he said, "for it may overcome any or all of the others; provided that will is made one with the pattern, see?" The pattern is in Jesus. Edgar Cayce continued, "For no influence of heredity, environment or whatnot surpasses the will; else why would there have been that pattern shown in which the individual soul, no matter how far astray it may have gone, may enter with Him into the holy of holies?" (5749-14)

Tom Sugrue, who wrote *There Is a River,* asked a question about the Christ Consciousness and the answer to it is very succinct and direct: "Should the Christ Consciousness be described as the awareness within each soul, imprinted in pattern on the mind and waiting to be awakened by the will, of the soul's oneness with God?" The answer: "Correct. That's the idea exactly!" (5749-14)

I am given to describing the soul as a three-faceted operation with mind—divine mind—and spirit and divine will. This is the energy pattern that was created as a soul. We were all created like this, all at once, long before the earth came into existence, according to Edgar Cayce's point of view. The soul had mind and spirit and will. The spirit is the energy of life, the energy pattern, and the will is the ability to choose the direction. The mind is the builder. It can build anything you move toward.

Now we have seen, we have heard, we know that the Son represents or signifies the Mind.
He, the Son, was in the earth-earthy even as we—and yet is of the Godhead.
Hence the Mind is both material and spiritual, and taketh hold on that which is its environ, its want [wont?], in our experiences.
Then Mind, as He, was the Word—and dwelt among men; and we beheld Him as the face of the Father.
So is our mind made, so does our mind conceive—even as He; and IS the Builder.
Then that our mind dwells upon, that our mind feeds upon, that do we supply to our body—yes, to our soul!      1567-2

The mind becomes the builder, and the patterns of our thoughts *build*. In response to a question about fasting, Edgar Cayce once said that it would do a whole lot more good to fast from some of the negative patterns of thought that were being held to. Food was not hurting near as much as the thoughts were. Fasting is a discipline of the *mind*. You've got to make up your mind before you can stop your hand from reaching for the food, of course. And fasting can also be abstaining from negative thinking so that we do not build negative patterns.

But as He manifests—as a portion of that Godhead that is represented in thee, as *in* thy Mind—then ye become aware that ye are *indeed* a child of the living God, and are in materiality for those purposes of manifesting those very things that are the fruits of the Spirit in thy dealings with thy fellow man.      1348-1

That's why we're here, according to the readings. We are here in materiality for manifesting the fruits of the Spirit in our relationship with each other. Now and then we make it difficult for each other, but it's still what we've got to do—and we need to get at it.

Know that as the Mind is represented by the Christ Consciousness, it is the Builder, it is the Way, it is the Truth, it is the Light; that is, through the manner in which the Mind is held.                                                             1348-1

This is the major pattern—the pattern to end all patterns.

. . .would that all would learn that He, the Christ Consciousness, is the Giver, the Maker, the Creator of the world and all that be therein! And ye are His, for ye are bought with a price, even that of passing through flesh as thou that He might experience and know all thy thoughts, thy fears, thy shortcomings, thy desires, the dictates of the physical consciousness, the longings of the physical body. Yet He is at the right hand, *is* the right hand, *is* the intercessor for ye all. Hence thy destinies lie in Him. . .

. . .He *is,* He *was,* He *ever will be* the expression, the *concrete* expression of LOVE in the minds, the hearts, the souls of men.

. . .He will guide thee, for He hath given His angels charge concerning those that seek to be a channel of blessing to their fellow man; that purge their hearts, their bodies, of every selfish motive and give the Christ—*crucified, glorified*—a place in its stead.                                             696-3

As given, each finds self most in the application of that it knows concerning the Father's and the Christ's ways in the hearts and lives of others. Not so much self-development, but rather developing the Christ Consciousness in self, being selfless, that He may have *His* way with thee, that He—the Christ—may direct thy ways, that He will guide thee in the things thou doest, thou sayest. [The readings are talking here about a very down-to-earth, everyday level of activity. They continue:] In this manner may one give of self to others most. Not as self-exaltation, but as glorifying the Christ that the Father may give those good gifts to those that love His ways.
                                                                281-20

How are we going to do this? Perhaps we'll admit it's a good idea—but we know it's hard, a lot of work, and how are we going to do it? "Replace," Edgar Cayce says, "animosities, hates and fears, with faith, hope, long-suffering, patience and with the purposes not merely of self, but of self applying the principles of the Christ Consciousness." (5046-1) It is *applying the principles,* and he states it again, "Then, as we find, there should be first the general mental attitude of manifesting the fruit[s] of the spirit as set forth by many of those in the application of the Christ Consciousness in the experience of the body. Practice, then, brotherly love, kindness, patience, long-suffering, gentleness." (3580-1)

How do we do it? Somebody once asked in a reading, "Is any entity, living or dead, maliciously attempting to put obstacles in my way?" Obviously, someone was bugging this person!

The answer was, "Only so far as resentments are held by the self towards others, as has been indicated. And if such as cause hate, malice, jealousy, fear and doubt are removed from thy own mind towards others, no influence without or within may be of a detrimental force to self. . ." (2081-2)

Nothing can affect you unless you build the attraction for it: unless you hate, unless you fear, unless you resent, unless you persecute, unless you are filled with malice and jealousy. These attract, you see.

. . .so long as self will surround self with the thought and the ability of the Christ Consciousness, and then practice same in its dealings with its fellow man.

No need to proclaim it alone—but live same, daily.  2081-2

Another person was told:

If the entity will read or study or analyze how the Master treated children, young people, during His ministry in the earth, it will be seen how oft He used children, the young people, as the hope of the world, as to how unless each individual puts away those selfish desires which arise and becomes as little chidren, one may never quite understand the simplicity of Christ's faith. . .                    1223-9

And somebody asked, "How may we have the mind of Christ?" Every single one of you in a Search for God Study Group has read that answer in the opening chapter.

As we open our hearts, our minds, our souls, that we may be a channel of blessings to others, so we have the mind of the Christ, who took upon Himself the burden of the world. So may we, in our *own* little sphere, take upon ourselves the burdens of the world. The *joy,* the peace, the happiness, that may be ours is in *doing* for the *other* fellow. For, gaining an understanding of the laws as pertain to right living in all its phases makes the mind in attune with *Creative* Forces, which *are* of *His* consciousness. So we may have *that* consciousness, by putting into action *that* we know.                    262-3

Then, He has come in all ages when it has been necessary for the understanding to be centered in a *new* application of the same thought, "God *is* Spirit and seeks such to worship Him in spirit and in truth!"

Then, as there is prepared the way by those that have made and do make the channels for the entering in, there may come into the earth those influences that will save, regenerate, resuscitate, *hold*—if you please—the earth in its continued activity toward the proper understanding and proper relationships to that which is the making for the closer relationships to that which is in Him *alone*. Ye have seen it in Adam; ye have heard it in Enoch, ye have had it made known in Melchizedek; Joshua, Joseph, David, and those that made the preparation then for him called Jesus. Ye have seen His Spirit in the leaders in all realms of activity, whether in the isles of the sea, the wilderness, the mountain, or in the various activities of every race, every color. . .                    5749-5

Then the awareness in patience, for this entity, is to become more and more aware of thy relationship to the Creative Forces. Do not grow anxious because those about thee deny thy faith. Only live it and be it; not in finding fault with others, not in condemning others. For as we forgive, we are forgiven; as we condemn others, we are ourselves condemned. Thus in patience, condemn not, neither find fault; not condoning, not agreeing, but let thine own life so shine that others, seeing thy patience, knowing thy understanding, comprehending thy peace, may take hope. For such comes only from finding the presence of the Christ Consciousness in self.

Then, when the entity as an individual speaks so loud there is little to be said. Others seeing, will take hope and they, too, will more and more draw closer to the oneness of purpose; all do not think alike. All approach according to their own concept. Yet as others see, there is felt the influence for creative or destructive forces in the life. For it is the spirit, the purpose, the ideal with which ye think, ye speak, ye act, that will determine what the fruit of thy life, of thy thoughts, will be. If ye sow the spirit, in the seed of the spirit of patience, of love, of long-suffering, brotherly kindness, the lack of hate— but love, love in everything, then ye will find, as He has given, He the Master, Jesus, the Christ Consciousness, will abide with thee. He has attained the Christ Consciousness in giving of Himself. Though able in mental and physical to lay aside the cross, He accepted same, offering self as the sacrifice; that ye

might have an advocate in the Father. Thus are ye saved, by grace.
Then be gracious, be thankful. 3459-1

Let me close with a quote from Teilhard de Chardin. "Some day, after mastering the winds and the waves, the tide and gravity, we shall harness for God the energies of love and then for the second time in the history of the world, man will have discovered fire."

# THE WORK OF EDGAR CAYCE TODAY

The Association for Research and Enlightenment, Inc. (A.R.E.®), is a membership organization founded by Edgar Cayce in 1931.

• 14,256 Cayce readings, the largest body of documented psychic information anywhere in the world, are housed in the A.R.E. Library/Conference Center in Virginia Beach, Virginia. These readings have been indexed under 10,000 different topics and are open to the public.

• An attractive package of membership benefits is available for modest yearly dues. Benefits include: a bi-monthly magazine; lessons for home study; a lending library through the mail, which offers collections of the actual readings as well as one of the world's best parapsychological book collections, names of doctors or health care professionals in your area.

• As an organization on the leading edge in exciting new fields, A.R.E. presents a selection of publications and seminars by prominent authorities in the fields covered, exploring such areas as parapsychology, dreams, meditation, world religions, holistic health, reincarnation and life after death, and personal growth.

• The unique path to personal growth outlined in the Cayce readings is developed through a worldwide program of study groups. These informal groups meet weekly in private homes.

• A.R.E. maintains a visitors' center where a bookstore, exhibits, classes, a movie, and audiovisual presentations introduce inquirers to concepts from the Cayce readings.

• A.R.E. conducts research into the helpfulness of both the medical and nonmedical readings, often giving members the opportunity to participate in the studies.

For more information and a color brochure, write or phone:

**A.R.E., Dept. C., P.O. Box 595**
**Virginia Beach, VA 23451, (804) 428-3588**